PENGUIN BOOKS

The Penguin Book of Early Music

Anthony Rooley has specialized in the music of the European Renaissance and has established a reputation as one of the leading lutenists in Europe and America. He is founder/director of The Consort of Musicke which concentrates on the enormous repertoire for voice, lute and viols from the various European countries, but particularly has made a special study of music from the English Renaissance. Their extensive record production has received many international awards, and their twenty-one record cycle of the *Complete Works of John Dowland* is of particular significance. At present Anthony Rooley is preparing a book on John Dowland which interprets his work in the light of Elizabethan literature, philosophy and contemporary social appreciation. He broadcasts regularly for the BBC and for various European stations. He is married and has three daughters.

AWeight
May 1981.

The Penguin Book of Early Music

An anthology of vocal and instrumental songs and dances from the Renaissance (1480–1620)

Compiled, annotated and edited by Anthony Rooley · *Penguin Books*

Penguin Books Ltd, Harmondsworth, Middlesex, England
Penguin Books, 625 Madison Avenue, New York, New York 10022, U.S.A.
Penguin Books Australia Ltd, Ringwood, Victoria, Australia
Penguin Books Canada Ltd, 2801 John Street, Markham, Ontario, Canada L3R 1B4
Penguin Books (N.Z.) Ltd, 182–190 Wairau Road, Auckland 10, New Zealand

First published 1980
Published in Penguin Books 1980

Printed in Great Britain by Fletcher and Son Ltd, Norwich
Filmset in Monophoto Bembo
Music artwork by Clifford Caesar

To my mother, and in memory of my father

Contents

Acknowledgements

The debt I owe to the members of The Consort of Musicke who took part in the original 'Musicke of Sundrie Kindes' concert and recording project in 1974/5 will be immediately clear to those who attended the concerts or have listened to the recordings. It was an honour to work so closely with such skilled musicians, who have helped bring hitherto obscure music to life through artistic insight and fine performances. This book has been compiled – with their help – in the hope of stimulating further performance rather than as a contribution to musical scholarship.

Extensive projects need skilled administration, and here The Consort of Musicke owes an enormous amount to Francesca McManus. The continued support of Decca Records Limited, and more particularly the several acts of faith of Raymond Ware and Peter Wadland, has allowed The Consort to mature and develop at a steady pace.

Encouraging noises were forthcoming from various individuals in earlier days, when *Early Music* magazine was young: John Thomson, the editor, was especially helpful. Professor Howard Mayer Brown also supported me in a variety of ways. Financial assistance came from the Ella Lyman Cabot Trust in Boston, Massachusetts, who showed great understanding over inevitable delays. I hope they recognize this present book as a product of their help. Kind assistance has been given by the staffs of the Senate House Library, University of London and the British Library.

I have drawn freely on the work of several people who contributed to the repertoire of The Consort by providing new editions or re-working old ones from source material. To James Tyler I owe a general debt for encouraging a new attitude to the editing of early music and a healthy scepticism with regard to the veracity and accuracy of the modern printed page. Trevor Jones edited numbers 24 and 25 and composed the lute decorations for number 25. Many hours of devoted labour has been expended by Julian Creme on editing music for The Consort, and numbers 3, 5, 7, 11 and 21 reflect here a small part of his work.

Emma Kirkby read the typescript with care and made many helpful comments. My assistant, Belinda Caldwell, has been a constant support; she inherited the preparatory work from Janet Hansford and continued from this sound basis whenever I provided material. Special thanks for her patience and perseverance. Finally, my wife Carla has been a source of steadfastness over the several years of work that this book represents. Her unfailing belief that it would eventually be completed is now rewarded.

Introduction

This collection of twenty-five pieces from several countries of Renaissance Europe is a selection from a large personal anthology made over a number of years. It is a personal choice of what may be termed domestic music: music for the home or for the delectation of a patron and his family and friends. Some would certainly have been performed by professional musicians during the normal course of their employment but other pieces, perhaps the majority in this collection, were intended for the hands of amateurs. Do-it-yourself music-making spread in a big way in the early years of the sixteenth century; indeed it was fundamental to the new-found humanist ideals central to the cultural re-birth we know as the Renaissance period.

My original purpose in making a large anthology was for a series of concerts and recordings under the title 'Musicke of Sundrie Kindes', an umbrella label appropriated from a book of English lute-songs published in 1607. I wanted to present a view of all the important aspects of Renaissance secular music-making, using mostly hitherto unrecorded music and avoiding pieces already familiar as Renaissance 'lollipops'. Unknown composers and anonymous works were placed alongside accepted masters, and vocal music was thoroughly re-integrated with instrumental, to show that such distinctions have developed mainly in recent years for the convenience of modern scholarship. The dates 1480 and 1620 were chosen to represent an approximate beginning and end to the Renaissance period, and any music which was essentially intended for secular use was considered.

All the pieces in this volume can be heard on a disc released by Decca Records called 'The World of Early Music' (SPA 547). These performances have been lifted from the original 'Musicke of Sundrie Kindes' boxed set of four records (DSLO 12BB203–6). The instrumentations chosen for the recorded performance were not intended to represent a definitive solution, nor necessarily the best, but were chosen to use the forces at my disposal to the best advantage.

It would be quite wrong for us to nurse the idea that everyone in the sixteenth century spent their lives singing, playing and dancing or that domestic music was heard in every home. Such an idyll as depicted in Brueghel's 'Wedding Feast' of musical jollification of the peasantry must be regarded as exceptional. The arts of singing and of playing the lute or viol were certainly numbered amongst the important social accomplishments and graces, but only at the most refined levels of society. In *The Booke of the Courtier*, published in Urbino in 1528 and first available in English in 1561, the great chronicler of Italian court circles, Baldassare Castiglione, tells us:

> My Lords, you must think I am not pleased with the Courtier if he be not also a musician, and besides his understanding and cunning upon the book, have skill in like manner on sundry instruments. For if we weigh it well, there is no ease of the labors and medicines of feeble minds to be found more honest and more praiseworthy in time of leisure than it.

and also:

> I have understood that Plato and Aristotle will have a man that is well brought up, to be also a musician; and declare with infinite reasons the force of music to be very great purpose in us, and for many causes (that should be too long to

rehearse) ought necessarily to be learned from a man's childhood, not only for the superficial melody that is heard, but to be sufficient to bring us into a new habit that is good and a custom inclining us to virtue, which maketh the mind more apt to the conceiving of felicity.

We are clearly in elevated company, a very small élite bent on self-improvement. For their purposes of inner development, all the arts were fair game in aiding the courtier, or his lady, in their quest.

But although Castiglione was writing for his own circle, his book exercised an extraordinarily wide influence on the whole of Europe for at least a hundred years. In England in 1622, Henry Peacham published his *The Compleat Gentleman*, a manual which simply amplified the points first presented in *The Booke of the Courtier*. The fashion for self-improvement manuals spread from court circles to the gentry and outwards to the rising middle classes, whose business expertise brought new-found wealth and leisure. It became the main social aim of this new class to ape the fashions and tastes of the nobility. A Flemish improvement manual of the 1540s, aimed at merchants of Brughe and Ghent, included a little domestic scene which was the model of good conduct for a family of quality. After supper, as the tables were cleared, Joseph (the head of the house) asked Williken (the page boy) to bring the music part-books from the sideboard cupboard. Dame Cataline (the wife) was to sing the *cantus* and the two sons the *altus* and *tenor*, whilst Joseph himself would sing *bassus*. This little scene was reiterated innumerable times in sixteenth-century publications. Thomas Morley's famous opening to his *Plaine and Easie Introduction to Practicall Musicke* (1597) is a re-working of the same idea – Philomathes had been embarrassed by not being able to sing his part in a consort. All the gathered company whispered in wonderment, asking where had he been brought up since he lacked this essential social grace.

Similar accomplishment was also expected upon the lute and viol. Tutors for the lute, aimed at the middle-class amateur market, were printed from the beginning of the sixteenth century in Germany, and in England, late as ever, by the end of the century. One such tutor, by Thomas Robinson, published in 1603 and called *The Schoole of Musicke*, is laid out in the form of a dialogue – following the pattern of improvement manuals as well as Platonic dialogues – and all the usual claims of the improving quality of music are used to exhort the pupil to apply himself diligently.

The earliest surviving autobiography in the English language is by the private music tutor, Thomas Whythorne. His private thoughts and anecdotes give us some direct insight into the atmosphere of domestic music-making. Whythorne's position as music tutor to a wealthy family was not at all unusual, as we may discover from the title-pages and dedications of the English lute song-books. Most of these composers received regular payment for tutoring the children and probably the parents too. No doubt the musical entertainments in the household were in the hands of the paid professional musician, whose functions included integrating professional and amateur, able and otherwise, to reveal to the world that his patron had refined sensibilities and was an embodiment of Castiglione's perfect courtier.

But the composer of Renaissance domestic music often left no precise instructions for instrumentation, allowing for several equally desirable solutions. The freedom to make the best use of available resources is now, as then, one of its attractions. Certainly we need not feel bound by exacting historical considerations at the outset. The music in this book sounds well played on almost anything. I remember a roomful of some twenty music teachers improvising divisions on the *passamezzo antico*, using a variety of tuned percussion, a clarinet, a flute and three guitars. The effect was stunning – not through the expected bizarre cacophony, but because the music, good all-purpose music, survived.

An historically accurate performance is an ideal to aim for of course. In the Renaissance period the most highly prized instrument was the voice, whose words carried the meaning or intention. It was also the instrument given to man by God to sing His praises. Percussion instruments, the bagpipe and the shawm all jostled for the lowest place in the Renaissance hierarchy of musical instruments. Somewhere in the middle would be the instrument that soothed or aided contemplation. Of the wind instruments only the flute (or recorder) had a regular place in chamber music. Other wind instruments were reserved for special effects or circumstances. Bowed and plucked instruments were most favoured by Renaissance musical tastes to furnish the greatest quality and variety of music for domestic delight. These instruments, after the human voice, were the most expressive. In the playing of a good lutenist or viol-player words could almost be heard!

During the Renaissance period locality was a key factor in determining appropriate instrumentation. Under what circumstances or at what time and place were the original performances given? An inner chamber was as different from the banqueting hall as the courtyard was from the street. And then the occasion of performance would determine yet further the choice of instruments. The inner chamber could accommodate a handful of guests attuned to the latest trends in music and poetry, or an evening of private diversion. In the street, a feast or Saint's Day in full regalia contrasted radically with a mere market day. Such considerations largely dictated the choice of instruments in general. Points of detail would be decided by availability and expertise.

To pretend to an historical veracity, it is not enough simply to be armed with a crumhorn, a rebec, a couple of recorders, a tambourine and a harpsichord. Most of the music in this book could be played on that combination and it would be very good fun. But it would bear little resemblance to any point in history. Even playing a viol made in the eighteenth century in a Byrd consort poses a problem. That instrument, although fine *and* original, would be much less suitable than a viol made last year according to late sixteenth-century principles!

How far should we go in attempting historical accuracy? The joy of early music in general and this collection of pieces in particular is that you can go as far as you like, for it is like a journey where each station yields new delights. If you begin using this volume with a guitar, a cello, a clarinet and a wobbly soprano, you are on your way. You have started. The rest is simply a matter of time and inclination.

How to use this book

1. The music provides a basic plain text, with occasional examples of elaboration.

2. Part ranges are termed *cantus* for the top, *altus* for the second, *tenor* for the third, and *bassus* for the lowest.

3. A note for singers. All the vocal pieces in this volume happen to be appropriate for our modern SATB combinations. Music of the Renaissance, knowing vocal possibilities so well and requiring a conversational freedom in singing, avoided extremes of range. You should feel free to transpose according to your available forces.

4. The introductory essays set the music in context and point to some of the features in the pieces. Instrumentation suggestions usually begin by outlining those used on the recorded performance and then suggest other possibilities. These suggestions refer to Renaissance instruments only, but it is tacitly understood that the modern equivalents or approximations can be substituted at will. For example the guitar can replace all the members of the lute family; violins, violas and cellos substitute for the viol family; oboes and clarinets can supplement the flute and recorder; tuned percussion can tackle anything within their range. Experimentation and imagination will lead to interesting musical solutions which can embody the spirit, if not the letter, of authenticity!

Finally, suggestions for interpretation give only the briefest guide to a subject which would justify a whole book.

5. The use of lute tablature as a notation system is intended for lutenists *and* guitarists. All the pieces can be performed satisfactorily without the lute part. Lutenists will understand the tablature without difficulty, but guitarists should make the initial simple step of tuning down the third string a semitone to F ♯ (which gives the same open-string tuning relationship as the lute) and then put on a *capo tasto* at the third fret. The pitch is then the same as for a 'G' lute, and all the tablature is then playable on the guitar. I particularly want to encourage guitarists to do this, because it really does form an excellent *entrée* to the music of the period and is extremely rewarding. In the further reading list are works explaining lute tablature in more detail, but the principle is simple enough to be outlined here, and experimented with straight away. The horizontal lines represent the strings, with the top line being the highest tuned string on the instrument (in guitar notation ①). The letters represent the frets, with 'a' being the open string, 'b' the first fret, 'r' (= 'c') the second and so on. Thus tablature is a diagram of the fingerboard and the positioning of the fingers, and is a very simple, basic notation system.

6. Technical terms and the names of Renaissance instruments have been used freely and without definition; a glossary will be found at the end of the book. Ranges of instruments are included where appropriate.

7. A further reading list is provided for those many subjects which are only touched on, and these items should be available at most music libraries.

1. *Ich draghe de mütse clütse* Jacob Obtrecht

I wear my hat askew

Jacob Obrecht (1450–1505) was a contemporary of Josquin des Prés, and with him one of a circle of composers responsible for developing and refining the art of polyphony; he drew on the Flemish motet style, which represented the finest embodiment of polyphonic principles, in all his compositions. By being as much a master of *chansons* based on popular folk music as of music for church, Obrecht stands as an individual within his circle: no other contemporary composer draws on so much indigenous music-making and he is one of very few actually to set songs in the Flemish language (a language which he clearly enjoyed for its own rustic qualities), as well as the more usual French, the refined language of court circles. In *Ich draghe de mütse clütse* Obrecht wears his skills as lightly as he wears the hat in question, displaying as much polyphonic skill as in a high-flown sonorous motet. The piece may have had words but if so they do not survive: all we have is the title as an incipit to each of the parts. The jaunty tune in the *tenor* carries the title well and easily and suggests the survival of the Flemish folk tune within this polyphonic texture. Obrecht's compositional technique is as intriguing as it is subtle. He decides to leave the entry of the real tune until the fourth bar, but anticipates it by having the *cantus* quote the opening phrase. The *altus* and *bassus* move in the same rhythmic motion giving emphasis to the earthy nature of the tune. Here the heavy Flemish peasant humour is captured as well in music as in Brueghel's paintings.

Instrumentation

Apart from evidence in contemporary paintings of groups of instruments playing together we have very little information on the likely instrumentation for a piece of this kind. The witty character of the music must be preserved and almost any instrumentation will be effective which gives full rein to the cheeky humour. All the parts, whilst reflecting each other's character, are wholly independent and an obvious solution is to give each line a quite different instrumental colour so that the timbre will reflect the individuality of the lines: a treble rebec on the top and a bass rebec on the bottom will give the outer parts some sense of unification, while sandwiching two very different timbres in the middle, such as an emphatically plucked lute on the *altus* line with a cornemuse buzzing away on the tune in the *tenor*. The use of a reed instrument for the folk tune helps the ear identify with the core of the composition. The nimble sound of the lute lightens the texture considerably and the reedy sound of the rebecs maintains the rustic vigour. All these instruments have a rhythmic precision which would not be present if a combination of flutes and viols were used. However if one thinks of 'wearing a hat askew', winding down a country lane without a care in the world, and whistling a jaunty tune in a carefree manner, this softer and more persuasive sound of flutes and viols would be appropriate. In the end the solution depends on the arranger's concept of the characterization.

Suggestions for interpretation

Decisions concerning articulation and phrasing will depend on the instruments finally chosen, but the natural vigour of the lines should not be smoothed out by too sustained a style of playing. Upbeats should on the whole be quite light and there should be reasonable separation between the minims. For contrast one could create a nice temporary suave effect in bars 13–17 by making the four minims in each part very *legato*. The notes tied across a strong beat should be held for their full value. In the duets when the syncopations occur at the same time the whole piece has a marvellous rocking feeling for a moment. When all parts move together, as in bar 40, the players need to agree on the comparative length and weight of each of the crotchets. In the triple-time sections the accents should be made quite clear, though care should be taken not to hurry the basic *tactus*. The direct simplicity of the style would suggest that there should be no *ritardando* into the final note: the piece can be allowed to settle by holding the final note itself for as long as seems necessary.

Cantus
Altus
Tenor
Bassus
10
20

30
40

70
80

2. *La La Hö Hö* Heinrich Isaac

Like so many Flemish composers of the late fifteenth century Heinrich Isaac occupied a position of international importance. His trans-European travels took him over the Alps into Italy where he was held in high esteem by the Florentine court under the patronage of Lorenzo de Medici; later, and for the greater part of his working life, he was patronized by Maximilian I in Austria. His polyphonic skills, as one would expect, may best be seen in his sacred music, most notably in his year-long cycle of works called *Choralis Constantinus*, which, incomplete at his death, was finished by his German pupil, Ludwig Senfl. Such a work on such a broad concept remains unique in church music.

The fine character-piece we have here, *La La Hö Hö*, is at the opposite end of the scale of Isaac's works. Here he presents with beguiling skill a musical distillation of tickling laughter, in four completely independent parts, though occasionally with a brief duet between parts. He begins with a theme, the tickle that starts it all off. Each bar opens with the same motif in close imitation, with entries at one-bar intervals. The top three parts then elaborate a little on the joke they have shared but the slow-witted bass is content to repeat the joke no less than eight times before the saucy midway cadence in bar 32! As the second half begins the bass starts up yet again with his stuttering as he repeats himself, but to our great relief, in bar 41, he bursts into new melodic material and contends with the rest in the same flight of syncopated fancy, and then there is no holding him back. At times it would seem as though the intention is to try to trip up or confuse the other parts as the syncopations mount in intensity. It is only in the final cadence that peace is wholly restored, with a final reiteration of the opening motif in the *altus*.

Instrumentation

The two most important considerations must be the independent characters of the parts and the humour of the music. The piece can be well played on four crumhorns, the intrinsic humour of these instruments being wholly appropriate, although the overall homogeneity would then reduce the characterization. On the other hand, four completely different-sounding instruments might well separate the texture out too much. One very congenial solution would be to use two each of such instruments as rebecs and lutes. Both are capable of great rhythmic precision, an essential feature if the syncopations are not to become wayward.

Suggestions for interpretation

Since the opening motif is used as a reference point throughout the piece it is essential to decide upon the precise articulation of every note in the phrase. Very short crotchets would give the theme maximum clarity in view of its constant repetition, with a good strong accent on the first note to make an incisive entry. Short notes should all be played very lightly and in every case leading towards the next long note. Syncopations should be more sustained than other notes, whilst dotted notes can be allowed some space. The cadence of bar 32 is too delicious to pass by lightly and though it poses considerable ensemble problems it would be most effective to work on a really quite indulgent *ritardando*. The *fermata* should be obeyed and perhaps held a whole minim beat extra, as in such an energetic piece a moment's rest for drawing breath is helpful both for the player and the listener alike. If the *altus* is inclined, the final quiet tickle could even be elaborated on the final note, as though one were loath to finish.

Cantus
Altus
Tenor
Bassus
10

20
30

40
50

3. *Je ne fay plus* Antoine Busnois / Anon. / Francesco Spinacino

Je ne fay plus, je ne dis, ne escrips, en mains escrips l'on trouvera mes regrets et mes plains.	I do no more, say no more, nor do I write, in many a writing you will find my regrets and complaints.
De larmes plains ou le moins mal que je puis le descrips.	Full of tears, that is the least I can say about it.
Toute ma joye est de soupirs escrips en dueil et cris il est a naistre a qui je m'en plains.	All my joy is written in sighs, in sorrow and weeping, he has yet to be born, he to whom I can complain.
Sil mes sens ont aucuns doulx motz rescriptz, ils sont parscriptz. Je passe temps pars desers et mes plains,	If my feelings gave rise to any sweet words, they are now no more. I spend my time in regrets and complaints,
et la me plains d'aulcunes gens plus traistres quant escris.	and I lament for I am betrayed.
Je ne fay plus, *etc.*	I do no more, *etc.*

The authorship of this beautiful French *rondeau* of the late fifteenth century is contested by different scholars today, though the majority are now in favour of the fine *chanson* composer Antoine Busnois. *Je ne fay plus* is a very fine example of the fifteenth-century *rondeau 'forme fixée'*. The poetic forms arising from the poetry of the Burgundian courts were of a highly stylized nature and the art of repetition was developed considerably, so that once a poem began to unfold it had to conform to a set pattern of repetition in its various parts. This formality of structure in poetry had to be followed in the setting of the poetry to music. Of all the forms in use at the end of the fifteenth century, the *rondeau* survived the longest and remained an inspiration to composers even when they were experimenting with much freer forms of *chanson*. The concept of endless repetition is somewhat alien to the modern way of thought, but beyond possible initial boredom the listener discovers a rich world of contemplation, presumably the same that was so deeply enjoyed in the fifteenth century. By repetition and familiar ritual in art one could find a new sense of freedom. The timeless quality of *Je ne fay plus* assures the piece a place amongst the greatest songs. It was common practice in the late fifteenth century to have the *rondeau* as a three-part texture; the vocal line could be in either the *cantus* or *tenor*, whilst the *bassus* was almost unvocal. However, as the century drew to a close it became increasingly common to write *rondeaux* in four parts and indeed, as the fashion ousted three-part writing, it became common to write a '*si placet*' part which could be added or not according to the performer's wishes. Sometimes, as in the case of the *si placet* which survives for *Je ne fay plus*, the part is created at the cost of considerable compositional barbarisms and for this reason is not included here. On the other hand, the beauty of this *chanson* ensured wide circulation throughout Europe and frequent adaptation, often of artistic distinction. For example a version for solo voice and lute survives in the earliest Italian lute manuscript, where the vocal line is as the original top line, but the lute part is a highly embellished reworking of the two lower parts. Also in Italy, found in the very first printed lute book by Francesco Spinacino (1507), there is a version of *Je ne fay plus* for two lutes in which the second lute plays an intabulation of the two lower parts of the original *chanson*, leaving the first lute free to play a rambling inspired embellishment based essentially on the top line but frequently ranging through all the parts. Such a line as this would easily have been improvised by one of the famed travelling virtuosi of the late fifteenth century who found patronage in the northern Italian courts. All three versions, the original three-part one, the version for solo voice and decorated lute, and the lute duet, are included here. The style of writing in the three-part version is appropriately languid for the mournful text; the words contain a familiar expression of unrequited love in which the singer feels that all inspiration is now denied him. In order to express these 'dolefull drerements' the vocal line starts out with long phrases which get longer as the two sections of the work proceed, so much so that in the B section the singer is required to vocalize on long held syllables as he enjoys his plaint to the full. The vocalized melismas are a particular feature of this style and contribute to the 'timeless' quality. The *tenor*, which could equally take words if one wished, has equal melodic importance, though in this particular instance it does not have quite the same melodic maturity. At times it syncopates against the top line and at times moves in parallel, as in the duet opening the B section which is particularly effective for its changing motion. Taken overall however the *tenor* tends to be a little more syncopated and a little more instrumental than the *cantus*. The *bassus* is on the whole the slowest-moving part, providing a firm foundation for the flights of fancy in the upper parts, though it is not denied rhythmic involvement at key points, such as bars 23–25 and the final six bars. The combined effect of the three parts is one of extraordinary refinement, matching the exquisite miniature paintings found in contemporary Books of Hours.

Instrumentation

The voice is clearly of utmost importance, the ideal choice being a soprano or a tenor with a clear and straight production. Declamation of the text must be the first consideration, ideally using a fifteenth-century French pronunciation (see further reading list for modern textbooks on this subject). For the three-part version one could use a soprano on the *cantus* and a tenor on the *tenor*, but it would also be appropriate to use a tenor on the *cantus* singing the line down an octave, despite certain points where the tenor would sound lower than the bass. Since the text is probably intended to be sung by a man (though this is not explicitly stated), there is preference perhaps for the tenor voice, and this is very effective in the version for solo voice and lute. The reflective nature of the work requires gently singing instruments, and a flute or tenor recorder on the top line with two viols (tenor and bass) on the lower parts would give a perfect balance; but in addition the decorated lute-duet part gives an exotic feeling to the *chanson* when incorporated with the other parts. One could experiment with different combinations of these possibilities in the course of one performance, though an original performance would probably have stuck to one instrumentation throughout a particular *rondeau*.

Suggestions for interpretation

The style of playing must be sustained and *legato*, to suit the lamenting nature of the text. The music attempts no word-painting but embodies the essence of the text, and the languishing sighs of a complaining lover should be in the mind and heart of the player when considering articulation and phrasing. At all times phrases should be dovetailed in the most graceful manner and the final cadences of each section should die away into silence. A sense of contemplation should pervade the overall style.

A
Cantus
Tenor
Bassus
Je ne fay plus,
je ne dis,
n'es - crips,
en mains es -
-crips l'on trou - ve - ra mes
re - grets et mes plains.
10
20

Rondeau A1 B1 A2 A1 A3 B2 A1 B1

A1 Je ne fay plus, etc.

B1 De larmes plains, etc.

A2 Toute ma joye est de soupirs escrips
en dueil et cris
il est a naistre a qui je m'en plains.

A3 Sil mes sens ont aucuns doulx motz rescriptz,
ils sont parscriptz.
Je passe temps pars desers et mes plains,

B2 et la me plains
d'aulcunes gens plus traistres quant escris.

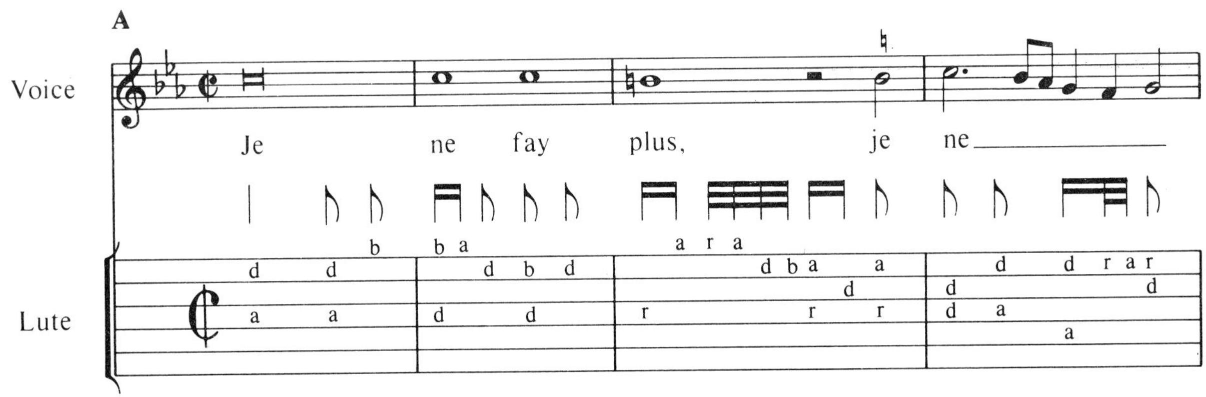
A
Voice
Lute
Je ne fay plus, je ne

dis, n'es - crips,

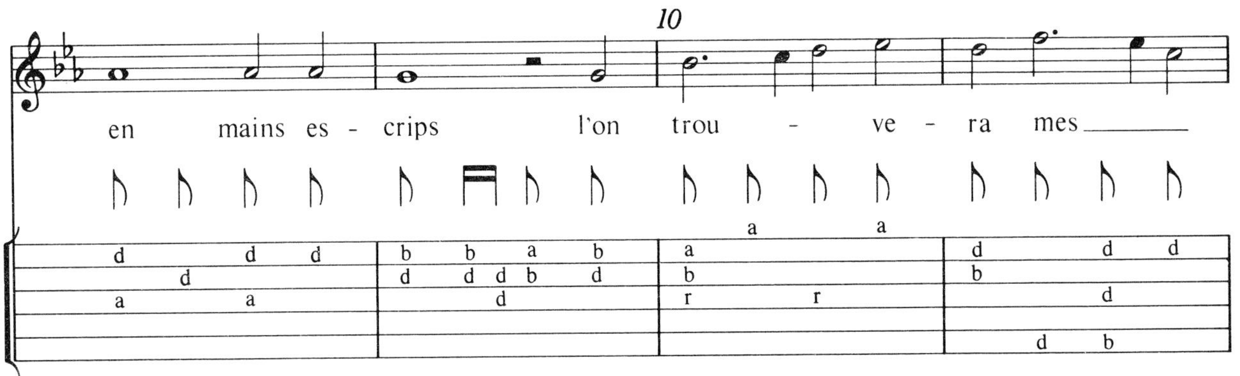
10
en mains es - crips l'on trou - ve - ra mes

re - grets et mes plains.

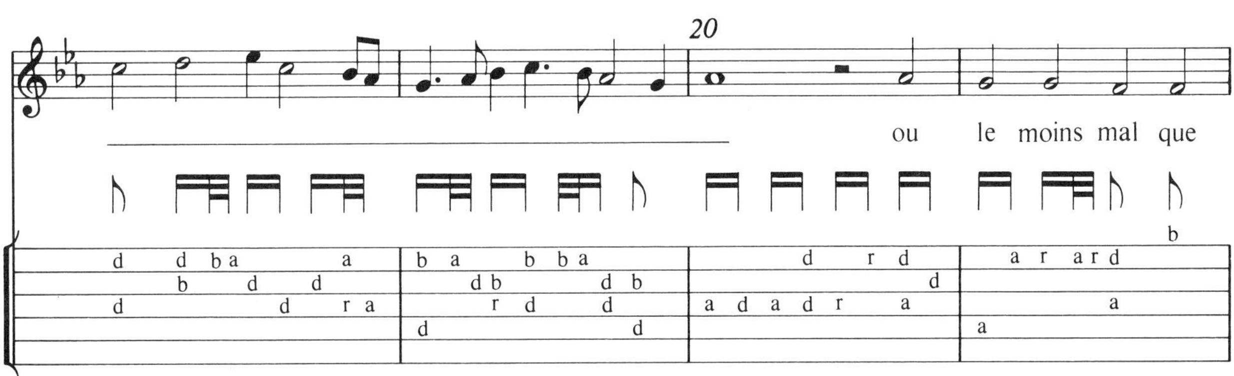

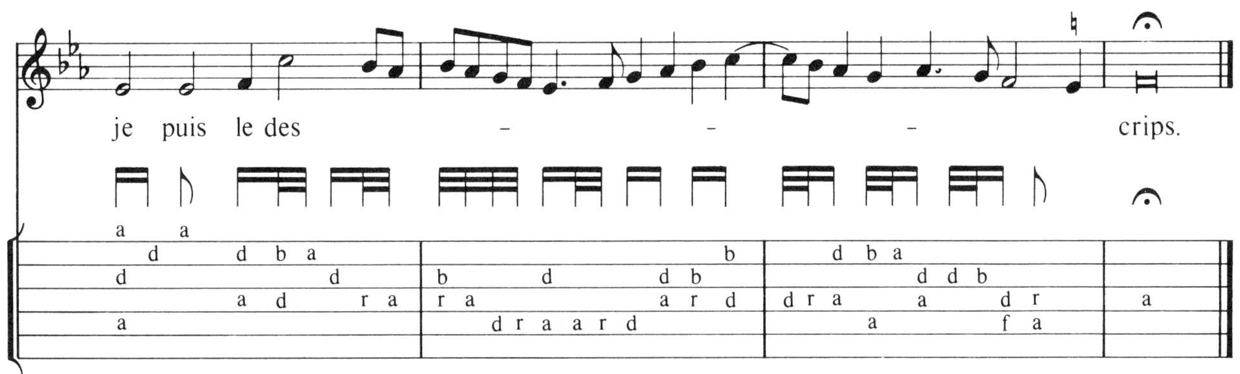

Rondeau A1 B1 A2 A1 A3 B2 A1 B1

A1 Je ne fay plus, etc.

B1 De larmes plains, etc.

A2 Toute ma joye est de soupirs escrips
en dueil et cris
il est a naistre a qui je m'en plains.

A3 Sil mes sens ont aucuns doulx motz rescriptz,
ils sont parscriptz.
Je passe temps pars desers et mes plains,

B2 et la me plains
d'aulcunes gens plus traistres quant escris.

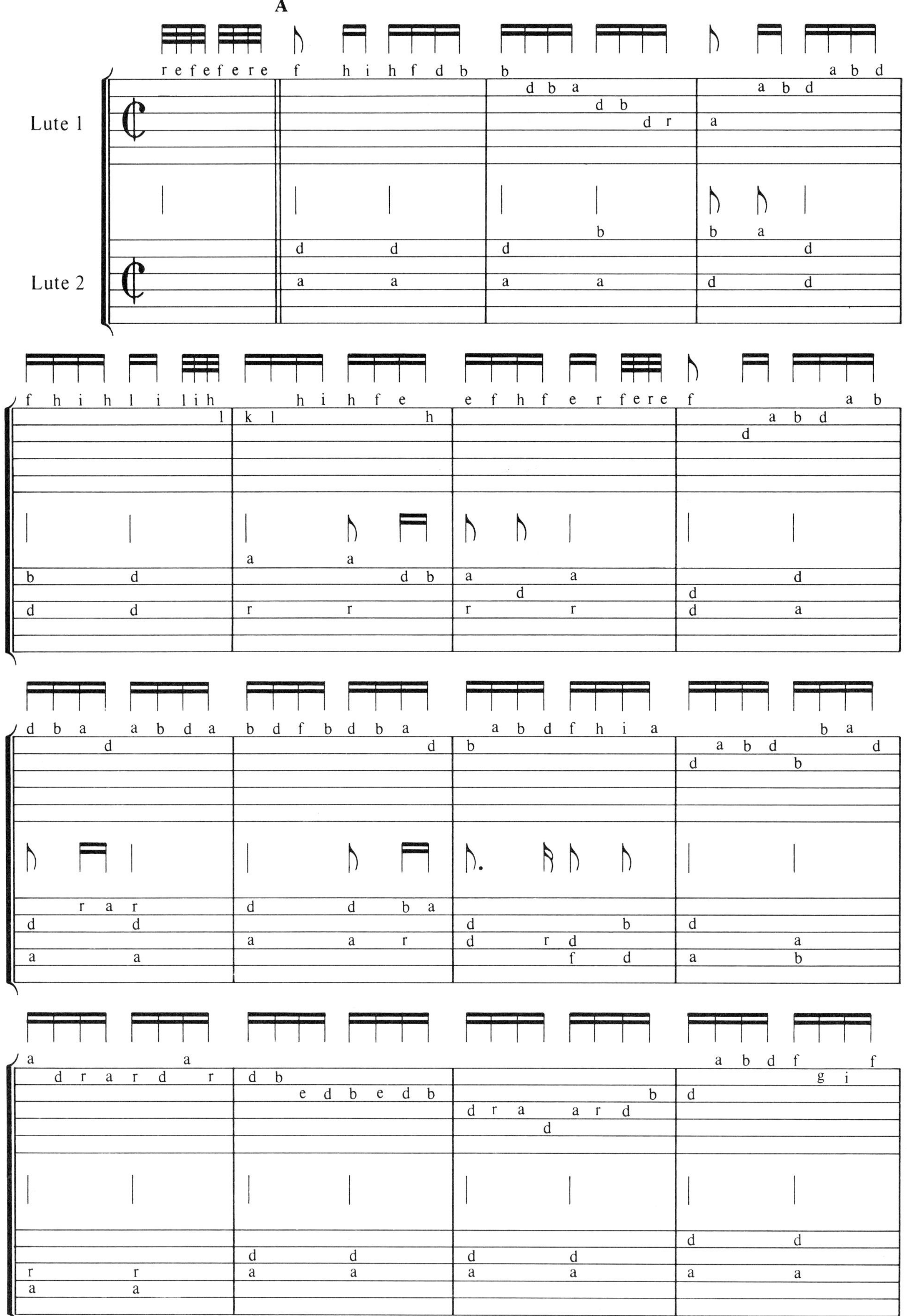
A
Lute 1
Lute 2

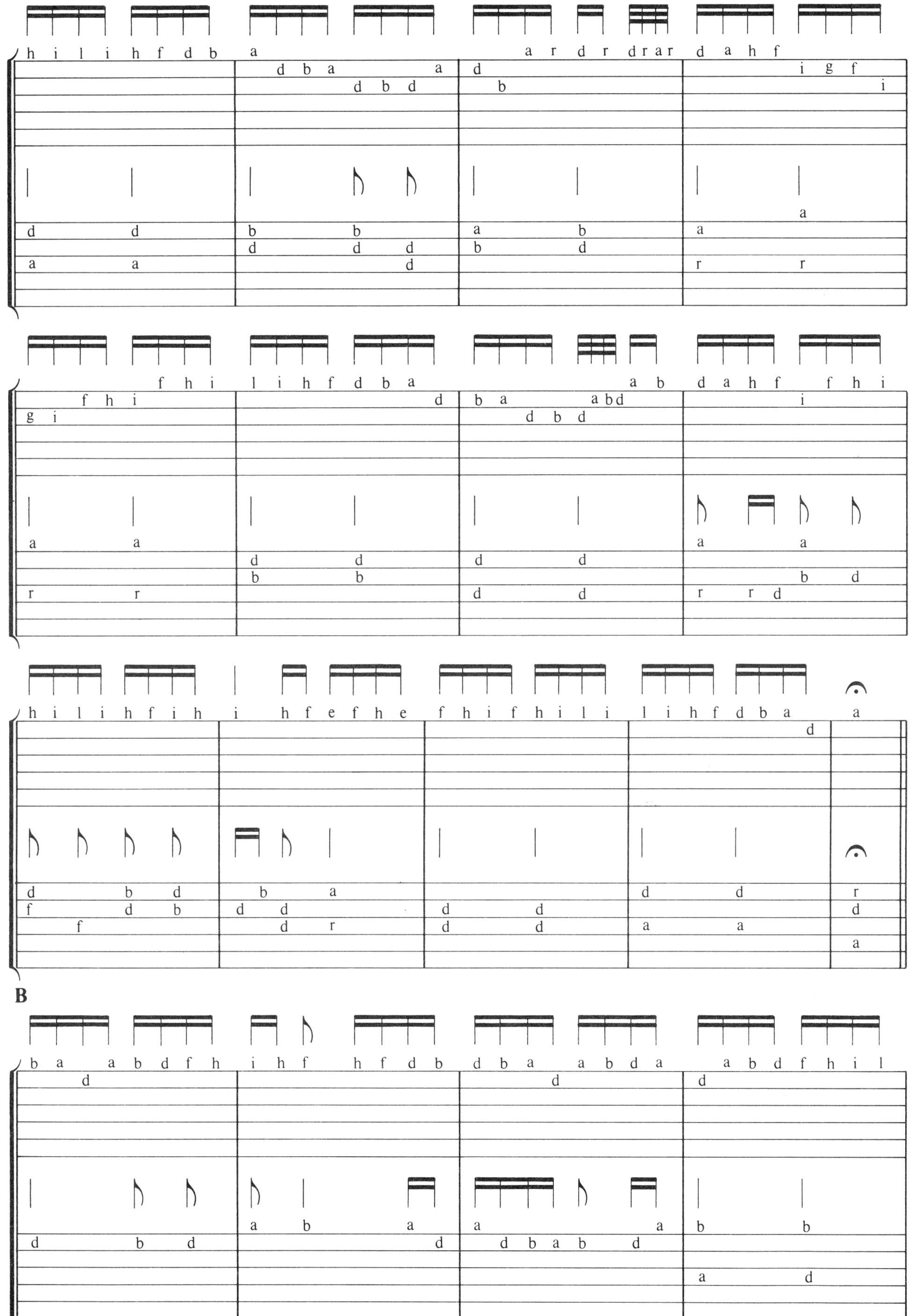

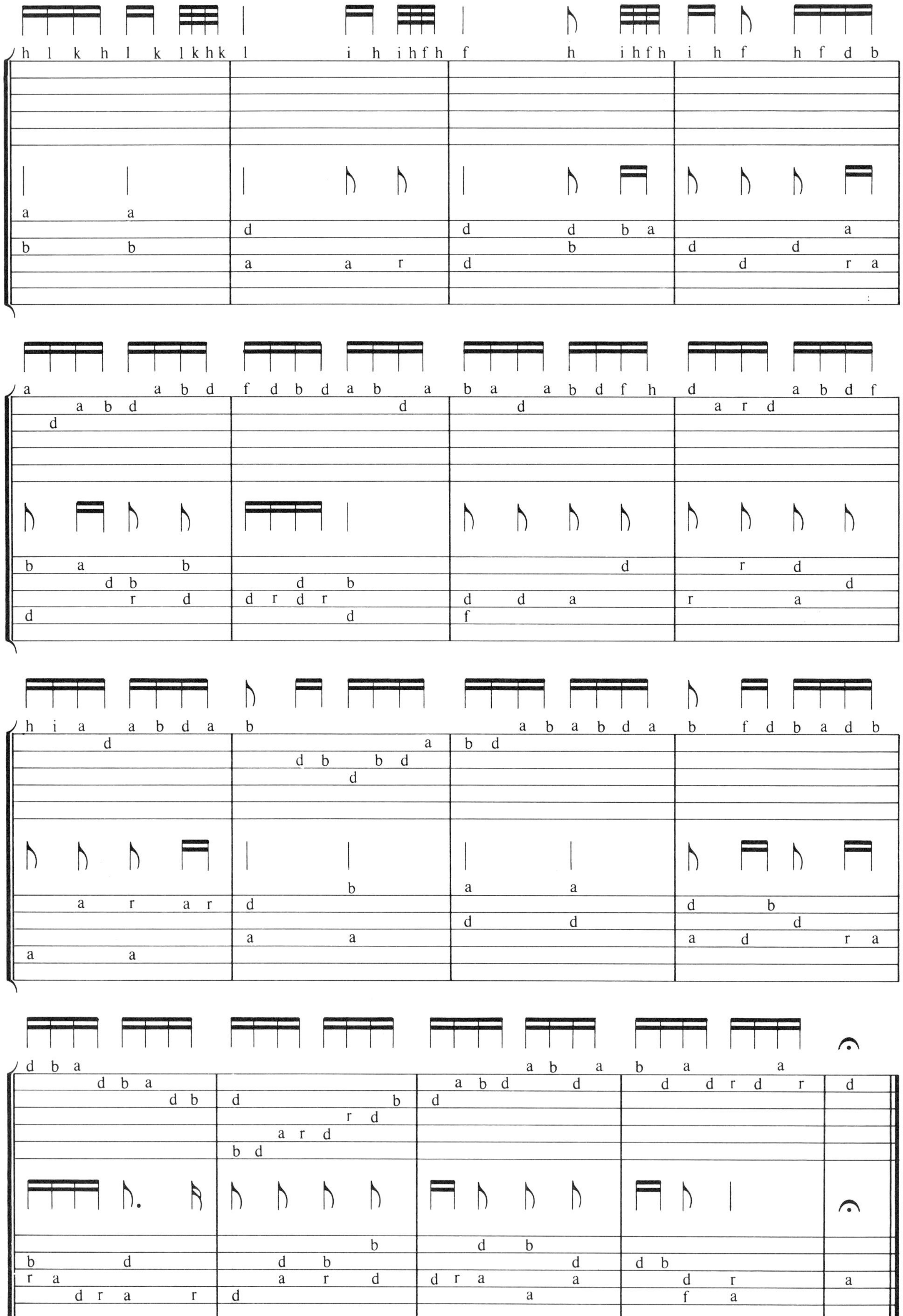

4. *Ostinato vo' seguire* Bartolomeo Tromboncino

Ostinato vo' seguire	Steadfastly I shall pursue
la magnanima mia impresa.	my noble enterprise.
Fa mi amor qual voi offesa	Love hurts me as much as you do,
s'io dovessi ben morire.	so I might as well die.
Ostinato vo' seguire	Steadfastly I shall pursue
la magnanima mia impresa.	my noble enterprise.

The Italian equivalent of the French *chanson* of 1500 was the *frottola*, a word which was used to describe a variety of poetic forms found in Italian poetry at the end of the fifteenth century. The new awareness of the possibilities of the Italian language (particularly the Tuscan dialect) played a considerable part in the development of the literary ideals encouraged in the major Italian courts of Urbino, Ferrara, Mantua and Florence. In particular the court of Isabella d'Este at Mantua was host to a new indigenous art which combined both poetry and music. Bartolomeo Tromboncino, her resident court-composer, played an active role in setting poetry written for and by Isabella for the delight, entertainment and improvement of the court circle. Much of the poetry was influenced by the Platonic ideals of love, beauty and truth, but the performer was not expected to emphasize his learning and dexterity; he had instead to appear as though inspired in the moment of performance – indeed art had to conceal art. In the little song *Ostinato vo' seguire* we have a prize example of the lively and overtly popular style of the *frottola* form known as *barzaletta*. The irrepressible vivacity of the song hides the fact that the text does not have very much to say. With persistence the singer feels he may win his love-suit, and has little more to tell us than that, but the charm and grace of the song beguile us and we are content to enjoy his sweet nothings.

Instrumentation

Most of the *frottola* repertoire was intended for performance by a single voice (soprano or tenor unless transposed to alto range) with instrumental accompaniment. It would seem from literary evidence of performance practice that the singer would have accompanied himself on either the lute or the *lyra de braccio* (as in this version), though the Italian word *lyra* may be used to mean any bowed string instrument, such as the viol. In the publications of *frottola* material it was normal practice for a song to be printed in four parts with the tune and words in the *cantus* and the three lower parts without words to be played by instruments. The style is essentially simple and homophonic with only occasional use of imitative procedures, in contrast to Flemish music where imitation and other compositional devices abound. The lute accompaniment would seem to have been the prime inspiration for the composer, and to have been the basis for the separate parts produced later for formal publication.

Suggestions for interpretation

The whole approach must suggest an improvisation of the moment. There must be no sign of tension or calculation. Furthermore, performing the notes is only a part of the story, for whenever there is a cadence of any kind it should be suitably embellished. The art of embellishment and gracing as appropriate for this music requires much deeper study but the important thing is to feel free to experiment, particularly with melodic division style of ornamentation. The final *'impresa'* is so written as to suggest that the lover, overpowered by his emotions, is brought to a condition of stuttering as he attempts to express his final word. The little hiccups should be enjoyed in this line. The nimble lute player requires to have the long descending scale towards the end of the piece 'in his fingers' in order for it not to catch him out.

O - sti - na - to vo'___ se - gui - re
la ma - gna - ni - ma___ mi - a im - pre - sa.
Fa mi‿a - mor___ qual voi of - fe - sa
s'io do - ves - se___ ben mo - ri - re. O - sti -
-na - to vo'___ se - gui - re la ma - gna - ni - ma___

30
40
mi - a im - pre - sa, la ma - gna - ni - ma mia im -
-pre - sa, im - pre - sa, la ma -
-gna - ni - ma mia im -
- pre - sa.

O - sti - na - to vo'___ se - gui - re
la ma - gna - ni - ma___ mi - a im - pre - sa.
Fa mi a - mor___ qual voi of - fe - sa
s'io do - ves - se___ ben mo - ri - re. O - sti -
- na - to vo'___ se - gui - re la ma - gna - ni - ma___

mi - a im - pre - sa, la ma - gna - ni - ma mia im -
- pre - sa, im - pre - sa, la ma -
- gna - ni - ma mia im -
- - - - - - -
- pre - sa.

5. *Pavana and Piva Ferrarese* Giovanni Ambrosio Dalza

The sources of Italian instrumental music of the latter half of the fifteenth century are extremely sparse. Though we know that dance music was greatly enjoyed as functional music for court dancing, nothing of this repertoire survives intact, mainly because of the improvisatory nature of dance music at the time. We have a series of treatises by various dancing masters describing Italian '*balli*' in some detail and they give the barest musical outline to go with the dance steps described. Despite considerable editing and arranging (even composing) there is nothing in this repertoire which can be used, so we are left in the frustrating position of knowing about the unbridled vitality of Italian dancing at the time and having only the merest sketch of the music. Fortunately we can find a few hints of what this music must have sounded like, in one of the earliest lute-solo publications printed in Venice in 1508. The composer Giovanni Ambrosio Dalza is a shadowy figure and his publication is somewhat enigmatic in that he devotes much precious paper to giving variant versions of two suites of dancing pieces, the *Pavana, Saltarello* and *Piva Veneziana*, and the *Pavana, Saltarello* and *Piva Ferrarese*. Each dance appears in a variety of keys for solo lute and with each transposition he varies the figurations, perhaps to show a lutenist how different embellishments fall reasonably easily to hand in different keys. Whatever his purpose for printing these transposed dances might have been, it gives us considerable information about his attitude to decoration practices and allows us to reconstruct, from the music he gives for solo-lute versions, dance pieces for ensembles. The music printed here consists of the *cantus* and *bassus* as Dalza gives it, with an added middle part drawn from the harmonies which he indicates, and some additional melodic movement according to the style of the other two parts. In addition two new lute parts are provided which give harmonic support and help to fill out the rather thin texture of three-part writing; a tenor lute in G and a bass lute in D are required for playing these parts. Only the *Pavana* and *Piva* of the Ferrarese Suite are included here.

Instrumentation

Dalza's version for solo lute does of course stand on its own, but the three-part version can be played on almost any instrumental combination. The arranger must choose either a loud dance ensemble (ideal for courtyard and open air) or a quiet ensemble appropriate for indoors. Two shawms and a sackbutt would provide the right tones for the first and would sound very exciting indeed. Alternatively two cornetts could be used in place of the shawms. With either of these combinations the lute parts are superfluous. On the other hand two recorders and a bass viol with one or both of the lute parts would sound very good for indoor use. The addition of a tabor, especially for the loud ensemble, would add to the rhythmic vitality and would aid the dancers considerably (the tabor should play the rhythm 𝅗𝅥 ♩ ♩/ 𝅗𝅥 ♩ ♩ for the *Pavana* and ♩. ♩. / ♩ ♪♫♫| for the *Piva*).

Suggestions for interpretation

Nothing should impede the obvious vigour of this dance music, and there should be an overall sense of really good fun. Within the endlessly long *cantus* line there are some phrasing breaks which will help to give shape and balance: the merest hint of a comma after the third beat of bars 2, 4, 6, 12 and so on will help bring balance and direction to the line. The lute parts are suggestions only and may be departed from according to the taste and preference of the player. Equally divisions can and should be introduced in the other parts, especially the *cantus*. Melodic ornamentations rather than trills would be more appropriate.

Cantus
Altus
Bassus
Lute 1
in G
Lute 2
in D

10

40

50

60

10

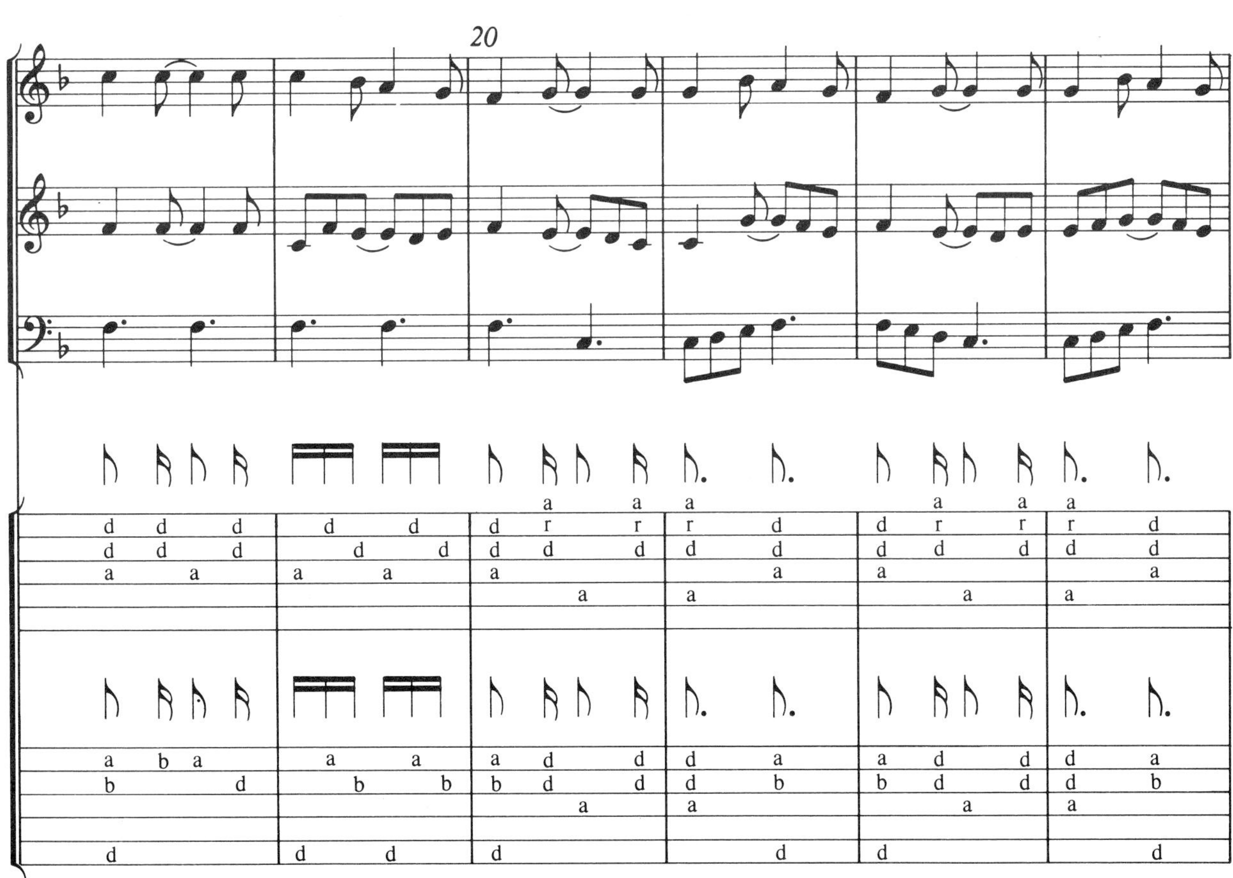
20

30

40

50

6. *Hor che'l ciel e la terra* Bartolomeo Tromboncino

Hor che'l ciel e la terra e'l vento tace
et le fere e gli augelli il sonno affrena,
notte'l carro stellato in giro mena
et nel suo letto il mar senz'onda giace.

Veggio, penso, ardo, piango, e chi mi sface
sempre m'inanzi per mia dolce pena;
guerra è il mio stato, d'ira ed di duol piena,
e sol di lei pensando ho qualche pace.

Così sol d'una chiara fonte viva
move'l dolce e l'amaro ond'io me pasco;
una man sola mi risana e punge.

Et perché'l mio martir non giunga a riva,
mille volte il dí moro e mille nasco;
tanto da la salute mia son lunge.

Francesco Petrarch

Now that heaven and earth and the wind are silent
and sleep holds fast wild beasts and birds,
night drives abroad her starry chariot
and in its bed the sea lies still.

I stare, I worry, I burn, I weep, and she who hurts me
is for ever before me, for my sweet sorrow;
my condition is like war, full of anger and pain,
and only when I think of her do I find any solace.

Thus from the same clear living source
spring both the sweetness and the bitterness on which I feed,
the same hand both heals and wounds me.

And to prevent my torment from reaching the shore
a thousand times a day I die and am reborn;
so far am I from my salvation.

Francesco Petrarch's poetry experienced a great revival *c.* 1500, particularly at the court of Isabella d'Este. His delicate and refined Tuscan dialect was regarded as the finest of Italian dialects and was chosen by fifteenth-century poets such as Pietro Bembo as the model for imitation. The sonnets of Petrarch were deemed to be the most perfect of that form, not only by the court of Isabella but by all educated Italians through to the beginning of the seventeenth century, and a text such as *Hor che'l ciel e la terra* can be found set by Italian madrigal composers from Bartolomeo Tromboncino to Claudio Monteverdi. Indeed, studying the settings of this one text through the sixteenth century reveals the changing fashion and fortunes of the Italian madrigal itself. Whereas Monteverdi draws from the poem the utmost sense of desolation, Tromboncino is satisfied with creating a mood of generalized resignation. Instead of accentuating individual words he creates a paradoxical experience of time standing still whilst ever-changing. The almost constant minim movement in the *bassus* makes for a formal and resolute *tactus* against which the fleeting *altus* and *tenor* parts turn. The words are equally resolutely declared in the top part. Tromboncino's judgement of the vocal phrase-lengths matches the poetic lines perfectly, and the music lies well for the voice: the effortless ease with which it unfolds helps delineate the agony of the text almost more realistically than word-painting. By the use of E♭ in bar 31 in the final coda the piece is brought to a quietly brooding close.

Instrumentation

The *frottola* format, of which this piece is an example, allows several possibilities of instrumentation. A lute playing the lower two parts would be quite adequate to accompany the voice. Certainly the lighter poetic forms such as the *strambotto* and *barzaletta* benefit from this simple solution, whereas the more grave forms of the *sonetto* and *ballata* perhaps benefit from a fuller accompaniment. The voice part can be sung quite effectively at either octave (by soprano or tenor voice), and the lower three parts can be played on three viols (two tenors and a bass) such as we find in some illustrations almost contemporary with the *frottole* repertoire. But on balance the evidence we have suggests the combination of a recorder or flute playing the *altus* line with perhaps two bowed instruments (preferably viols) playing the *tenor* and *bassus*. If desired the lute can be used to double these instruments, in which case it should be encouraged to play a few passing notes in its upper part.

Suggestions for interpretation

Building up from the *bassus* the ensemble should aim to create a mellifluous texture in order to support the voice, so the *bassus* line must be played in a beautifully relaxed style with *legato* minims providing the right foundation. When articulation is required the merest lift is enough, as for example on the second minim of bars 5, 9, 13 and so on. The *altus* and *tenor* need to be quite self-effacing, delivered with ease and grace. The same hairline space for phrasing as in the *bassus* will suffice for articulation. The treatment of dotted crotchets and syncopations generally will benefit from lightening the note towards its end, particularly in a descending line, and this will help the performer to play in a relaxed and easy manner.

Cantus
Altus
Tenor
Bassus
Hor che'l ciel e la ter - ra e'l ven - to
Veg - gio, pen-so, ar-do, pian - go, e chi mi
ta - ce et le fe - re e gli au - gel - li il son - no af-fre -
sfa - ce sem - pre m'i - nan - zi per mia dol - ce pe -
10
- na, not - te'l car - ro stel - la - to in gi - ro me - na et
- na; guer - ra è'l mio sta - to, d'i - ra e di duol pie - na, e
1
2
nel suo let - to il mar sen - z'on - da gia - ce. pa - ce. Co -
sol di lei pen - san - do ho qual - che

20
- sì sol d'u - na chia - ra fon - te vi - - - va mo -
per - ché'l mio mar - tir non giun - ga a ri - - - va, mil -
- ve'l dol - ce e l'a - ma - ro on - d'io mi pas - co; u -
- le vol - te il di mo - ro e mil - le nas - co; tan -
1 2
- na man so - la mi ri - - sa - na e pun - ge. Et lun - ge, tan -
- to da la sa - lu - te mia son
30
- to da la sa - lu - te mi - a son lun - ge.

7. *Ricercare à 3* Guilio Tiburtino

The early history of the development of idiomatic instrumental music has yet to be written. But the pieces by Tiburtino will undoubtedly occupy an important place in such a history. Before him, towards the end of the fifteenth century, some of the earliest purely instrumental non-dance music may be found in the *Glogauer Liederbuch*, together with songs and motets. There is a series of pieces intended, it seems, for purely instrumental performance, which are outstanding in their successful exploitation of idiomatic instrumental techniques. Immediately before Tiburtino and probably having direct influence on him, two Flemish composers, Johannes Martini and Heinrich Isaac, composed pieces which used various instrumental colourings to great effect. Both composers worked for several years in Italian courts, especially Martini who was employed as music tutor to Isabella d'Este. Tiburtino must have been influenced by the older Flemish composer, whose three-part solmization *ricercari* were influential in establishing a purely abstract instrumental fantasy-style. The syllables of the note-names (*ut*, *re*, *mi*, *fa*, *sol*, *la*), or solmization syllables, were given according to the opening motif or theme of each *ricercare* thus identifying each composition, hence Tiburtino's example here, 'la, sol, fa, mi, fa'. His skill lies in the fullest exploitation of the minimum musical material. The overall contemplative mood helps players and listeners plumb the depths of this beautiful cerebral activity. A geometric order begins to emerge, the aural equivalent of the visual weaving arabesques of the lute 'rose'.

Instrumentation

The broad musical structure suggests a homogeneous ensemble. The individual lines, though very alive and independent, reflect each other and the beauty of the texture is in its unity. Tiburtino gives us no direct instructions on instrumentation but his work was published in 1549, by which time we know that the use of complete consorts of instruments had become well established. The music will sound well on any three instruments of the same family, though its hidden subtleties would perhaps be made most apparent by those with the greatest range of tonal and dynamic colouring, that is the stringed instruments either bowed or plucked. Three viols come first to mind, though it would also sound very well on three lutes. If a whole consort is not possible then a recorder, lute and viol could be used. Oddly enough this is the sort of music which is sometimes claimed on title pages to be appropriate for singing or playing (*per cantare e sonare*) in which case the vocalist would presumably vocalize syllables on the notes, since no words exist. Such sounds as 'fa la la' or 'fa la li le la' appropriately placed on strong and weak beats would give a very interesting presentation.

Suggestions for interpretation

Most of the phrases in Tiburtino's style are fairly short but fluid. In this piece they are almost always descending, so the effect must be of the piece constantly flowing, becoming ever more relaxed as the phrase starts from a high point of tension and flows downwards to a point of relaxation. When a phrase does rise it rises against the general direction of the work and should therefore have a really positive strength. When all the parts are moving together a light *staccato* will help to avoid too dense a texture. An air of grace and space should be created during the performance.

Altus
Tenor
Bassus
10
20

30
40

50
60

8. *Sentomi la formicula* Filippo Azzaiolo

Sentomi la formicula su la gambetta, madonna mare sentomi, la fa la li le la.	I feel a tingling on my leg, my dear mother, I feel it, la fa la li le la.
Sentomi la formicula su la cusetta, madonna mare *etc.*	I feel a tingling on my thigh, my dear mother, *etc.*
Sentomi la formicula su la pancetta, madonna mare, *etc.*	I feel a tingling on my tummy, my dear mother, *etc.*
E se la senti fia, deh! sping' e para che la gh'andara.	And if you feel it, my dear daughter, go on, push on, it looks as though it will be fine.

Pure, unadulterated folk music or genuine, popular street music could not really be expected to survive from the sixteenth century. The ephemeral nature of folk culture guarantees that written documents could at best only hint at the oral tradition. However in the late 1540s and 1550s Filippo Azzaiolo set himself the task of collecting songs which were termed '*villotte*' (literally street-songs) and publishing them in versions which must only be one step removed from folk music. They have an overt simplicity, if not banality, but their very avoidance of melodic, rhythmic and harmonic invention gives them a special quality all their own. Often coarse and salacious, the words seem rather vulgar and as banal as the music. To fill out the versified doggerel, *vocalise* is used in a rather buffooning manner. Such sounds as 'fa la li le la' and 'fa ni nu na ni na na' were the sixteenth-century equivalents of 'bee bop a lu la' and 'dah bah dah bah doo'. In this case our text hints at being saucy without making itself too clear – it leaves much to the imagination, though other texts are explicit in the extreme. It is important to realize that this genre was not limited to Azzaiolo and the street level, for some of the finest 'art' composers of the period contributed to the style. *Villotte* were specially written for the delight of the court circles, and a composer of the stature of Orlando di Lasso even published a whole volume of such works.

Instrumentation

The forceful vigour of the music and the abruptness of the text requires an instrumentation which is equally direct. Four male voices – alto, tenor, tenor, bass – give the most direct delivery imaginable. Ideally these songs should be seen as the Renaissance equivalents of 'Rugby' songs, and delivered in the same lusty manner. The quiet instruments would be far too refined but of course such simple music *can* be performed with anything you have to hand.

Suggestions for interpretation

It may or may not be authentic but it is certainly effective to have the singers singing with broad nasal vowels, and as grossly as you can make your well-trained singers perform. Consonants may be spat out with considerable energy and particularly the 'fa la li le la' needs a little extra something. However, intonation is of crucial importance if all the voices are singing straight, nasal and without vibrato. Pure intervals are essential and this piece can in fact provide a very good exercise in basic vocal ensemble-singing.

A
Cantus
Altus
Tenor
Bassus
1.2.3. Sen - to - mi la for - mi - cu - la
1.2.3. Sen - to - mi la for - mi - cu - la

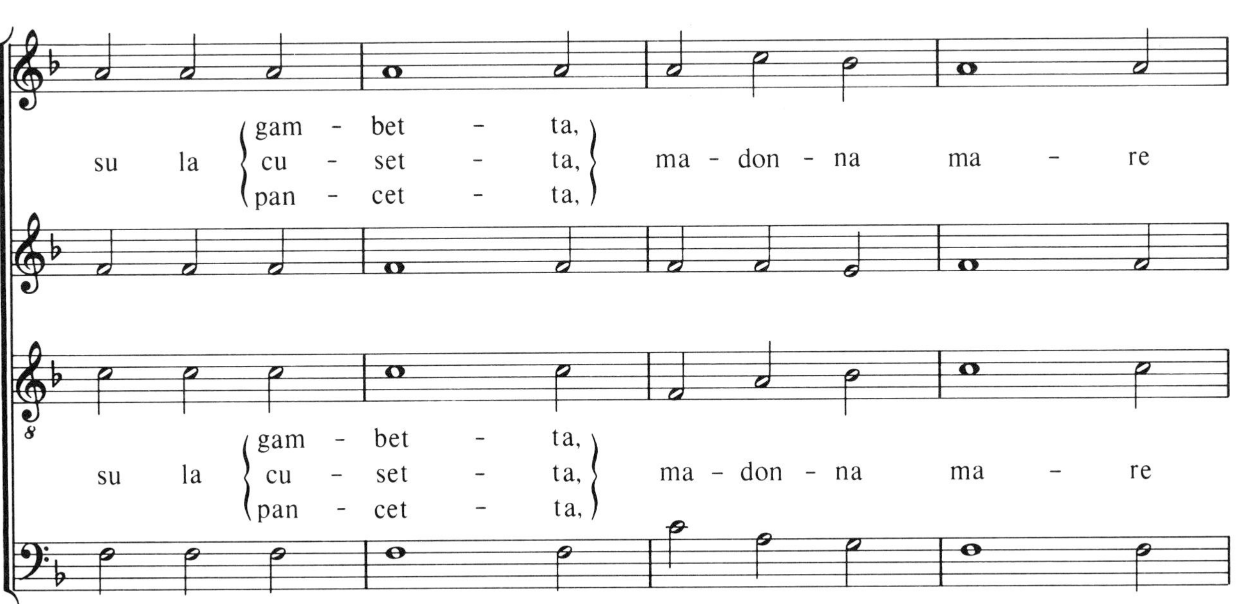
su la gam - bet - ta, cu - set - ta, pan - cet - ta, ma - don - na ma - re
su la gam - bet - ta, cu - set - ta, pan - cet - ta, ma - don - na ma - re

1,2
3
sen - to - mi, la fa la li le la. la.
sen - to - mi, la. la.
sen - to - mi, la fa la li le la. la.
sen - to - mi, la. la.

B

E se la sen - ti fi - a,
E se la sen - ti fi - a,
E se la sen - ti fi - a,
E se la sen - ti fi - a,

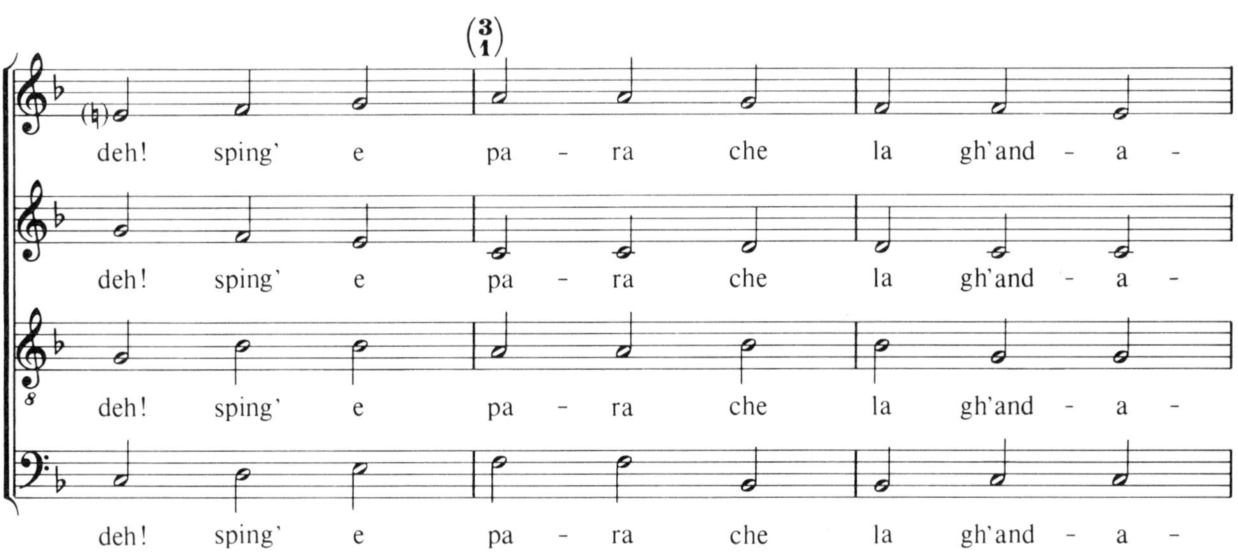
(3/1)
deh! sping' e pa - ra che la gh'and - a -
deh! sping' e pa - ra che la gh'and - a -
deh! sping' e pa - ra che la gh'and - a -
deh! sping' e pa - ra che la gh'and - a -

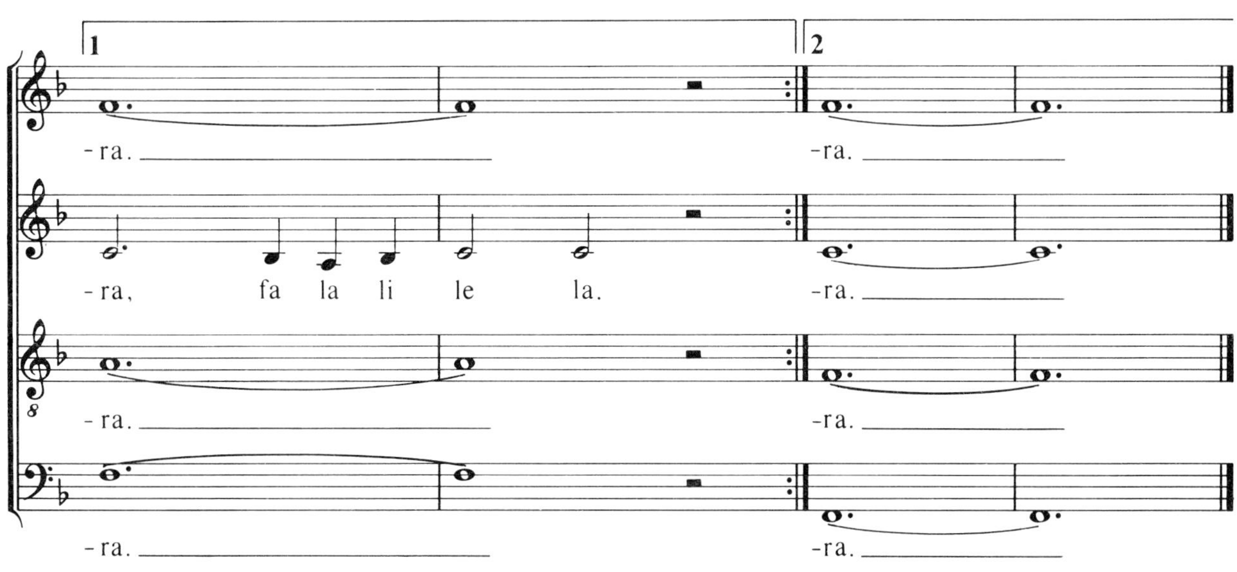
1
2
-ra. -ra.
-ra, fa la li le la. -ra.
-ra. -ra.
-ra. -ra.

9. *La bella Franceschina* Anon. / Pacolini

La bella Franceschina *ninina bufina,* la fili *bustacchina* che la vorria mari *nini*, la fili *bustacchi.* Lo suo padre alla finestra *ninestra bufestra* la fili *bustachestra*, ascoltar quel che la di' *nini*, la fili *bustacchi.*	Pretty little Frances, a young girl, wants a husband. Her father at the window listens to what his daughter is saying.
Tasi, tasi Franceschina *ninina bufina* la fili *bustacchina*, che te daro mari *nini*, la fili *bustacchi.*	Quiet, quiet, little Frances, my dear daughter, I'll give you a husband. I will.
Te darogio lo fio del Conte *ninonte bufonte,* la fili *bustaconte* del Conte Constanti *nini* la fili *bustacchi.*	I'll give you the son of the Count, my daughter, of the Count Constanti, my dear daughter.
E no vogio lo fio del Conte *ninonte bufonte,* la fili *bustaconte* del Conte Constanti *nini* la fili *bustacchi.*	But I don't want the son of the Count, the son of the Count Constanti I don't.
Che vogio quel giovenetto *ninetto, bufetto,* la fili *bustacchetto*, che sta in prigion per mi *nini* la fili *bustacchi.* Fa la li, fa la li le la, *etc.*	For I want that nice young man Who is in prison for me, I do. Fa la li, fa la li le la, *etc.*

(*N.B. All the words in italics in the original are meaningless jingles*

This piece is set somewhere in northern Italy between 1520 and 1580. Pretty little Frances, a 'doe-eyed innocent maiden', wants a husband and her father has ambitions to marry her into aristocracy because he knows her beauty is worth a penny or two. She has other ideas since she has fallen in love with a young man who is in prison because of her. The story is timeless and the tune likewise. They both belong wholly within the folk tradition. The banality of the story was recognized even in its own day since we find nonsense syllables attached to the end of each line, as though the singer were stammering, and these meaningless jingles sound very invigorating sung in a broad Italian dialect to give the song its humour and character.

Instrumentation

The tune had a considerable life and occurs in various settings for harpsichord, for four instruments and, in the first version we have here, for three lutes. Each lute on the first strain plays simply the tune and harmonies and then the higher two lutes play divisions which rattle against each other in a delightful way on the repeats: this is good basic dance music based on a folk tune. A variant version of the tune is used for the second, textual, version: lutes can improvise some kind of accompaniment.

Suggestions for interpretation

The three-lute version requires lutes tuned either in A, E and D or G, D and C. Probably the first combination would be the one favoured in Italy in the middle of the century. For the vocal version literally any accompaniment would be appropriate playing the harmonic sequences and improvising a few passing notes. The character portrayal will depend on the individual singer and his ability to portray pathos and humour. This piece can be played on two guitars as follows. The first guitar should tune the third string to F#, put a *capo* at the fifth fret, and then play the part for lute 1 in A. The second guitar should tune the third string to F#, use open tuning, and play the part for lute 2 in E. With the addition of the occasional bass note from the third lute part the piece will be complete as a duet.

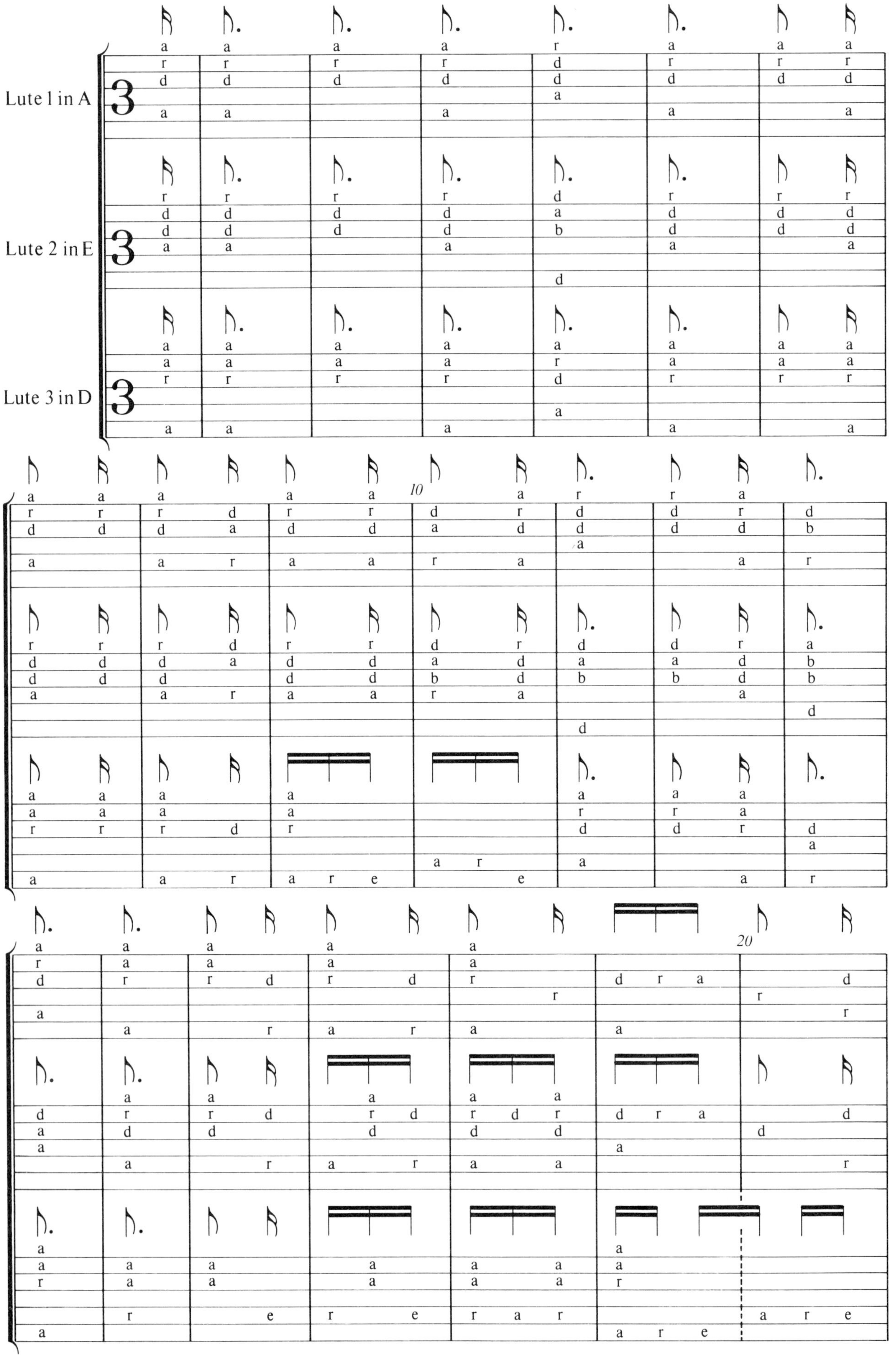

Lute 1 in A

Lute 2 in E

Lute 3 in D

10

20

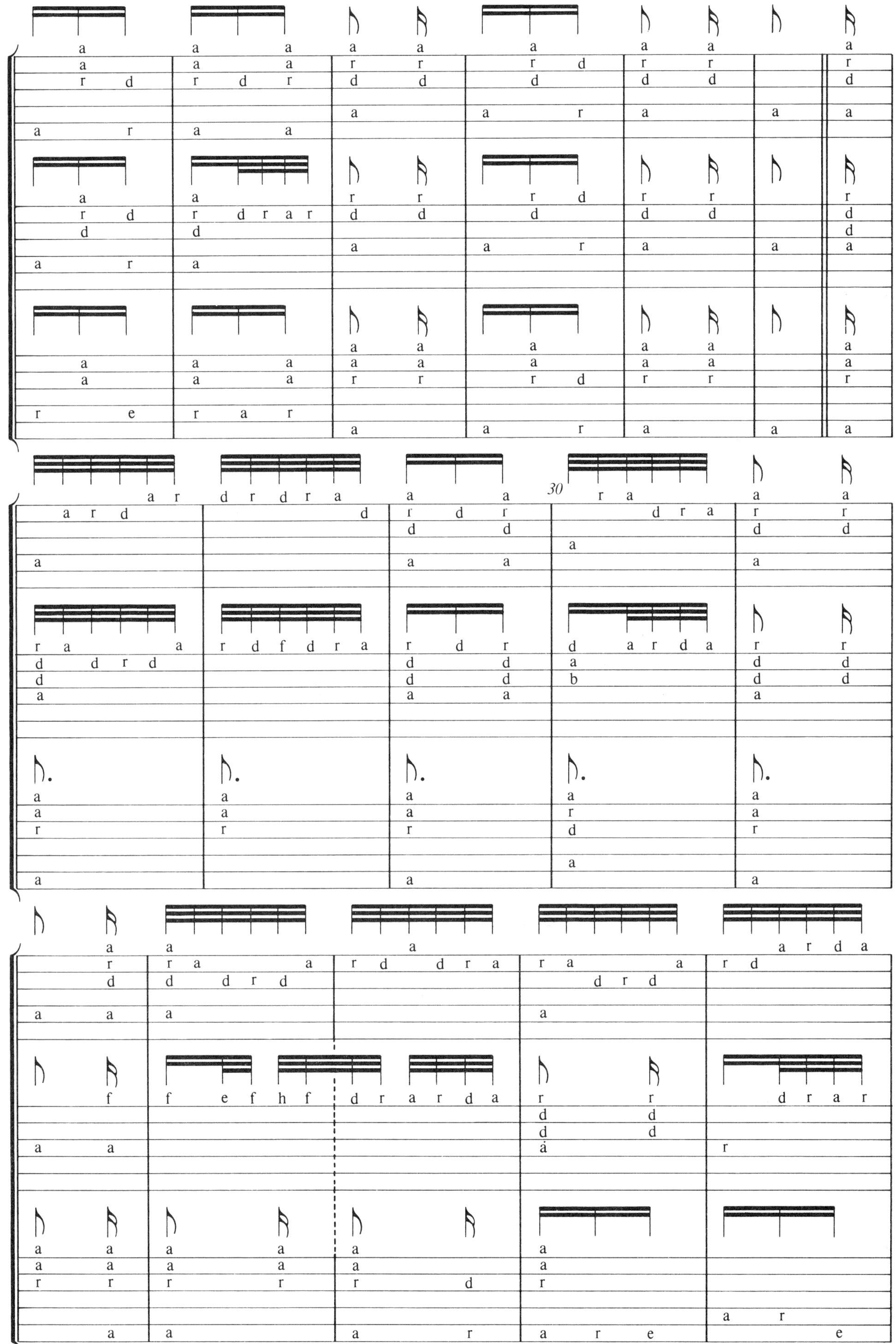

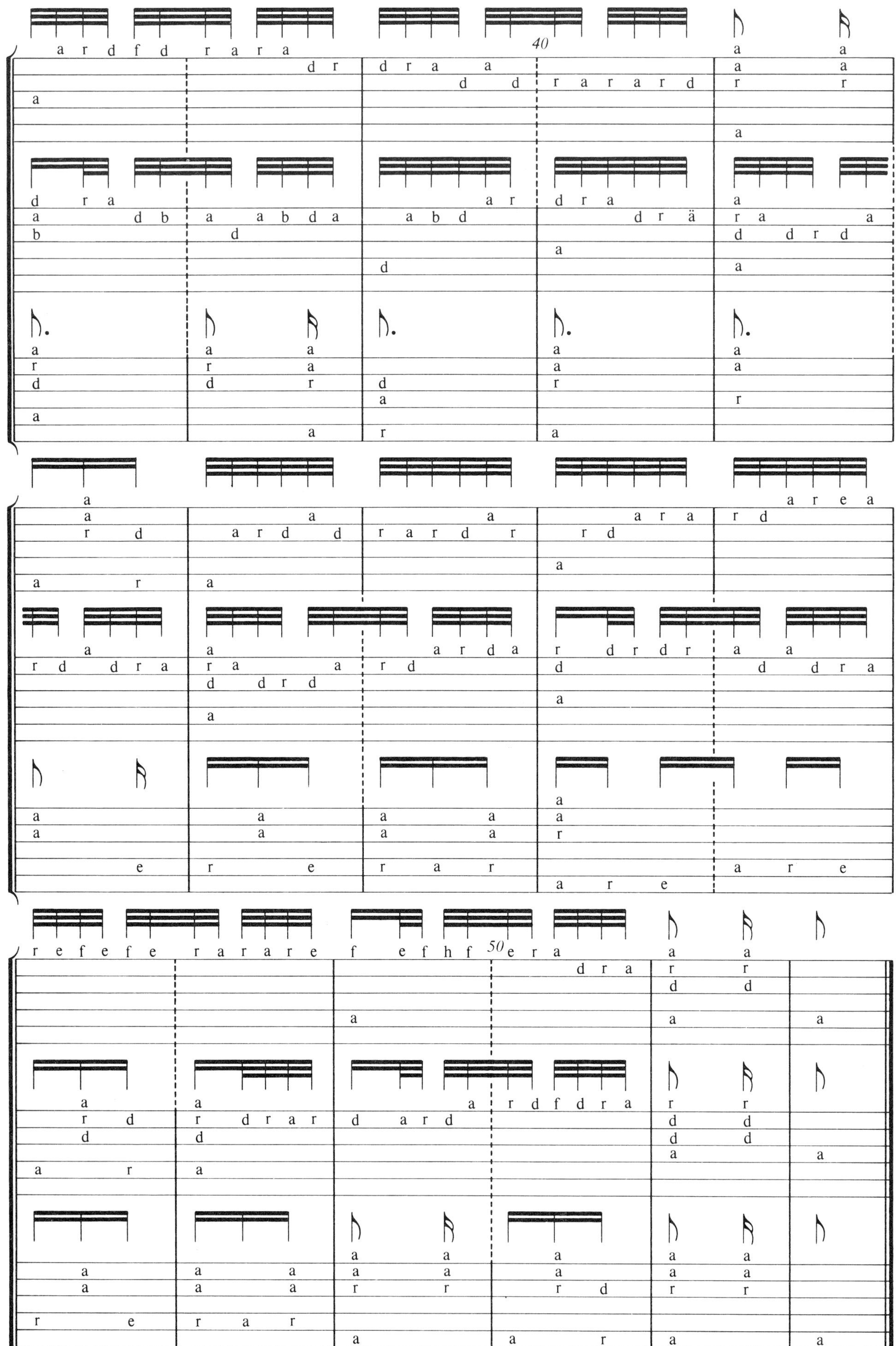
40
50

Lo suo padre alla finestra *ninestra bufestra*
la fili *bustachestra*, ascoltar quel che la di' *nini*,
la fili *bustacchi.*

Tasi, tasi Franceschina *ninina bufina*
la fili *bustacchina*, che te daro mari *nini*,
la fili *bustacchi.*

Te darogio lo fio del Conte *ninonte bufonte*,
la fili *bustaconte* del Conte Constanti *nini*
la fili *bustacchi.*

E no vogio lo fio del Conte *ninonte bufonte*,
la fili *bustaconte* del Conte Constanti *nini*
la fili *bustacchi.*

Che vogio quel giovenetto *ninetto, bufetto*,
la fili *bustacchetto*, che sta in prigion per mi *nini*
la fili *bustacchi.*
Fa la li, fa la li le la, *etc.*

10. *La Brillantina* Guiseppi Guami

The development of the Venetian *canzona* style was due almost entirely to the work of Andrea Gabrieli, organist at St Mark's, Venice. In the hands of his nephew Giovanni Gabrieli it was brought to full flower by the end of the sixteenth century. This specifically instrumental style, known as the '*Canzona Francese*', was Italy's greatest contribution to abstract instrumental ensemble music. An increasing number of composers worked in this form, one of the most outstanding being Guiseppi Guami who published his volume of *Canzone Francesi* in 1610. This contains mainly works in four parts with an accompaniment for keyboard instrument playing *basso seguente*, a style which led eventually to the better known *basso continuo*. Guami here specifically selects imitative entries for doubling – and hence strengthening – by the doubling instrument. *La Brillantina* opens with a rather sad little theme which is imitated in all parts giving a genuine polyphonic beginning, and for the most part the voices promise to be of equal importance. But as the work unfolds it becomes clear that the equality is being eroded. We witness here a step towards the breakdown of the sixteenth-century polyphonic tradition and the move towards the Baroque era, with its polarization of attention to the outer parts so that eventually the inner parts are lost all together, a development which leads directly to the trio sonata.

Instrumentation

Guami seems to be writing primarily for strings, and gravitating towards the bright sound of the violin family. This piece probably sounds most effective on two violins, viola and cello (preferably constructed and strung in accordance with data appropriate to 1600); as for the *basso seguente*, either a small chamber organ or a small Italian harpsichord would be ideal. Several other alternatives could be extremely satisfying. If the top part cannot be played on a violin then a flute could take its place with strings, or other quiet instruments, below. For a quiet ensemble it would be possible to use a theorbo or a chittarone for the *basso seguente*. A combination of cornett, tenor cornett and two sackbutts would also be possible.

Suggestions for interpretation

The players must agree on the articulation of the opening phrase which can very easily seem too stodgy, and the four crotchets should lead on to the minim, otherwise the work starts to plod. *Diminuendo* after playing the motif to allow other entries through without forcing. Adopt a relaxed and easy style which allows the music to speak for itself and articulate as much as possible to minimize the muddying effect of the crotchet movement in all parts.

Cantus
Altus
Tenor
Bassus
Basso seguente

10

20

30

40

50

11. *Nerinda bella* Raffaello Rontani

Nerinda bella,
posiamci un poco
in questo prato
di fiori ornato
ch'età novella
più caro loco
ne più giocondo
non ha nel mondo.

Lovely Nerinda,
let us rest awhile
in this meadow
dotted with flowers,
for in youth
we cannot find
a more pleasant place
or a happier one in the world.

Sì, sì, cor mio,
tra questi fiori
posiamci al ombra
ch'il caldo sgombra,
ch'io pur desio
temprar gl'ardori
tra queste aurette
così dilette.

Yes, yes, my beloved,
among these flowers
let us rest in the shade
which shields us from the heat,
for I too wish
to cool my brow
among these breezes
so delightful.

Quant'è adorno
d'ogni intorno
di cipressi e verdi allori
pare il nido
caro e fido
delle gratie e de gl'amori.

How beautiful the world
is all around us,
with cypress trees and laurels
it looks like the resting place,
beloved and true,
of graces and cupids.

Mira il fonte
su quel monte
ove nasce questo rio
per far bello
il praticello
par che dichi à voi l'invio.

Look at the spring
on that hill
where this stream is born
to make this meadow
so beautiful.
It seems to say: I am sending it to you.

Mira i gigli e i gelsomini,
mira i crochi e gl'amaranti,
e le rose se steggianti
com'adornano i confini

Look at the lilies and jasmine,
look at the crocuses and amaranth
and the jubilant roses,
how they adorn the borders.

Vedi i vaghi augelli
sopra gl'arboscelli
come lieti saltano.

See the pretty birds
on those branches,
how cheerfully they chirp!

Senti com'a schiera
nella primavera
dolcemente cantano.

Hear how they sing
sweetly all together
a springtime song.

Senti quel cardellino
come veloce
snoda la voce.

Hear that goldfinch,
how swiftly
it chirps and trills.

Cantiamo a gara
con questi augelletti,
qui l'ore passiamo
fra gioie e diletti.

Let's join in the singing
of these birds,
let's spend hours here
with joy and delight.

Senti quel rosignuolo
come lieto risponde al nostro canto.

Hear that nightingale,
how gaily it answers our song.

Odi la rondinella
come festeggia anch'ella.

Hear the swallow;
it too makes merry.

Cantiamo a gara, *etc.*

Let's join in the singing, *etc.*

Nerinda bella is one of those rare works so radiant that the sun seems to break through at the first chord. The Italian *arioso* style, here at its graceful best, is used to portray those qualities of innocence appropriate to young lovers. The idyllic pastoral, borrowed by the Renaissance from Theocritus, allows a rustic shepherd and his nymph in Arcady to see the world afresh. Around 1600 dialogues began to be used as a way of exploring dramatic expression; even in highly formal rhetoric a sense of realism is generated as the two voices unfold the 'argument'. Very often, as here, the story-line moves to a close which requires the two singers to duet together, bringing a richness and fullness of sound at the very end. This '*dénouement*' is very satisfying and many of the best Italian composers contributed to the genre. They had imitators in France and England even by 1610. Today the repertoire still remains to be explored.

Instrumentation

Rontani and his fellow composers understood the voice well, writing for it with a precise awareness of range, style and colour; therefore the only voices to be used here are soprano on the *cantus* and tenor on the second line. Light but expressive and responsive voices suit best. The accompaniment is of the *basso continuo* style and is required to be 'realized' by the players. A 'figured bass' is given in the original which indicates essential harmonies, chord positions and essential suspensions. All this must be filled out by the player. A harpsichord or spinet would be very suitable, although preference would marginally be given to the lute family: chitarrone, theorbo or lute. Some lively but graceful passing-notes would suit the mood of the piece. Suggested lute parts, accompanying each voice, are given in this style, but should not be regarded as part of the composition. Debate continues about the use of a bass viol to underpin the harmonies, but in my opinion the dialogue repertoire, being a little more dramatic and a little stronger than the solo song of the same time, benefits considerably from it.

Suggestions for interpretation

Clear enunciation of the text is essential; it is after all an exchange of words, and the listener must be able to participate in the exchange. The *tempo* should be moderate but lively, so the lovers have time to express their enthusiasm. Rontani marks trills, but doesn't indicate what type he would like; presumably light and simple turns which do not interfere with the flow are most appropriate. For the close, both singers must experiment with a mutual decoration that has a fulsome but not over-virtuosic effect. The accompaniment must be light, clear and incisive, and should follow the vocal phrasing. It is a minim, not a crotchet, pulse, and this will aid the lightness.

Cantus
Tenor
Bassus
Lute(s)
Ne-rin-da bel - la, po-siam-ci un po - co in ques-to pra - to di fio - ri or-
-na - to ch'e-tà no - vel - la più ca - ro lo - co ne più gio-con - do non ha nel
mon - do.
10
Sì, sì, cor mi - o, tra questi fio - ri posiam-ci al om-bra ch'il cal - do sgom -

-bra ch'io pur de-si - o tem-prar gl'ar-do - ri tra ques - te au-ret - te co - sì di-let - te.
Quan-t'è a-dor - no d'ogn - i in-tor-no di ci - pres - si e ver - di al - lor - i par-e il
20
ni - do ca - ro e fi-do del-le gra - tie e de gl'a-mo - ri, del-le gra - tie e

Mi-ra il fon - te su quel mon-te o - ve nas - ce ques - to
de gl'a-mo - ri.
ri - o per far bel - lo il pra - ti - cel - lo par che di - chi à voi l'in-vi -
- o, par che di - chi à voi l'in-vi - o.
Mi-ra i gi - gli e i gel - so-mi - ni, mi-ra i

cro-chi e gl'a - ma-ran - ti, e le ro - se se steg - gian - ti com'a - dor -
-na-no i con-fi - ni.
40
Ve - di i vaghi augel - li so - pra gl'arbos-cel - li
co - me lie-ti sal - ta-no.
Sen - ti com'a schie - ra nel - la pri-ma-

50
-ve - ra dol - ce-men-te can - ta - no, dol - ce-men-te can - ta - no.
Sen - ti, sen - ti quel car-del - li - no, co - me ve - lo - ce sno -
- - da la vo - ce.
Can-tia-mo a ga - ra, a ga - ra con
Can-tia-mo a ga - ra,
can-tia-mo a ga - ra con

60
ques-ti au-gel-let - ti, qui l'o - re pas-sia - mo fra gio - ie e di - let - ti.
ques-ti au-gel-let - ti, qui l'o - re pas-sia - mo fra gio - ie, fra gio - ie e di - let - ti.
4 3
Sen-ti, sen-ti quel ro-si - gnuo-lo co-me lie - to ris-ponde al nostro can - - - - - to.
6
70
Can-tia-m'a
O - di la ron-di - nel - la co-me fe - steg-gia an-ch'el - la.

ga - ra, cantia-m'a ga - ra, a ga - ra con ques - ti au-gel-let - ti,
Can-tia-m'a ga - ra, can-tia-m'a ga - ra con ques - ti au-gel-let - ti, qui
1.
2.
qui l'o - re pas-sia - mo fra gio - ie e di - let - ti,
l'o - re pas-sia - mo fra gio - ie, fra gio - ie e di - let - ti, qui

qui l'o - re pas - sia - mo fra gio - - -
l'o - re pas - sia - mo fra gio - - - -

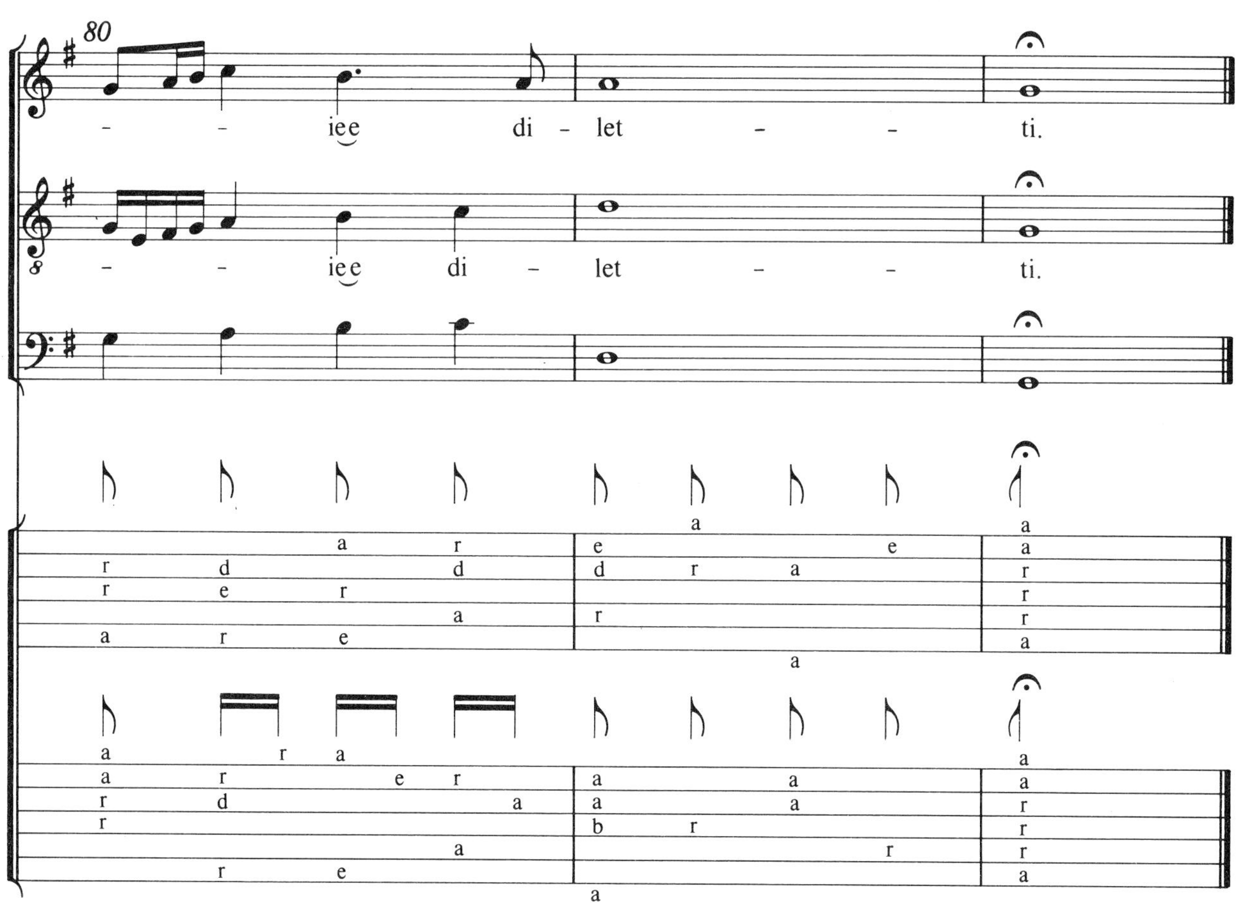
80
- - iee di - let - - ti.
- - iee di - let - - ti.

12. *Virgo celesti* Loysete Compère

Virgo celesti.
decorata partu,
semper humano generi miserta,
iugiter sese tibi dedicantes
aspice servos,
Virgo Maria.

Virgin,
graced with a heavenly child,
taking pity as always on humankind,
look on your servants
who dedicate themselves to you for ever,
Mary the Virgin.

Virgo celesti is a miniature masterpiece, condensed into twenty-eight bars yet a perfect example of the flowing Flemish motet-style of *c.* 1500. Despite the sacred text, the piece was probably never performed in church but intended for private devotional use. A highly mystical cult gathered around the worship of the Virgin Mary which was, in some instances, apparently tantamount to idolatry. This little work is actually constructed on a very carefully worked-out plan of number-symbolism dear to these esoteric gatherings. Briefly, its salient features are: there are twenty-eight *tactus* units (4 × 7 = the highest hopes of worldly [4] aspiration [7]) in a triple prolation (3 being the tripartite nature of God); the piece is in 5 parts (5 is the number of marriage or union [2, representing the female plus 3, representing the male equals 5] though this is unusual, four being more common); the *cantus firmus* consists of the six notes of the hexachord rising from D to B (6 being the number of the lover, or abundance); the words *virgo celesti* are reiterated to the *cantus firmus* on each of the three statements (3 being the most powerful number in prayer, once each for the Father, Son and Holy Ghost); there are six beats' silence before the *cantus firmus* is stated for the first time, four beats' silence before the second and two beats' silence before the last time; each time the *cantus firmus* is sung, the length of each note of the hexachord is reduced by one third: shortening both the rests and the time span of the theme has the effect of hastening or intensifying the heavenward prayer, achieving a powerful sense of elevation. Amidst all these numerological considerations, the piece maintains its quality simply as a fine piece of music. The art of the Flemish polyphonists was in achieving a balance between intellect and feeling. Compère's brief work is a masterful example.

Instrumentation

The polyphonic style is essentially a vocal style and an *a capella* performance would be entirely appropriate. However, the rhythmic vitality of the parts gives them an independence which allows for many instrumental solutions. The basic architecture is clearly defined by using the viols on the four outer parts and having a baritone voice enunciate the *cantus firmus*; thus the attention is drawn to the structure. This slightly unsubtle approach, whilst very effective, has the drawback of losing part of the text so a voice on the *cantus* or *altus* lines might be preferred. Whatever instruments are used they should strive for a seamless polyphonic style of phrasing.

Suggestions for interpretation

Rhythmic subtleties abound. Though the *tactus* is in three, often two units are combined so that 𝅝 𝅗𝅥 𝅝 𝅗𝅥 becomes 𝅝 𝅝 𝅝. Bring this out whenever an individual part allows it, especially when several parts move together in this manner (e.g. bars 17–18 and 19–20). The superb close must be handled with the greatest delicacy whilst maintaining the rhythmic vitality.

Cantus
Altus
Tenor 1
Tenor 2
Bassus
Vir - go ce -
- le - sti, de - co - ra - ta par - tu, sem - per hu -
Vir - go ce -
10
- ma - no ge - ne - ri mi - ser-
- le - sti,

- - ta, iu - gi - ter se - se
Vir - go ce - le -
20
ti - bi de - di - can - tes, a - spi - ce ser -
- sti, Vir - go ce -
- vos, Vir - go Ma - ri - a.
- le - sti.

13. *Belle, tenés moy/La triquotée* Anon.

tenor

La triquotée est par matin levée
sa pris sa harpe, au bois s'en est allée,
la triquoton, la triquoton, la belle triquotée.

The maid got up in the morning,
she took her harp and went into the wood.
The maid, the maid, the fair maid.

cantus

Belle, tenés moy la promesse
que vous me feistes pieca,
car jamais mon coeur ne fera
nouvelle amour n'autre maistresse.

My love, keep the promise
that you made me long ago,
for my heart will never feel
new love, nor take another mistress.

Si j'ay du mal j'aray léesse,
toutes les fois qu'il vous plaira.

I could be as happy as I have been miserable
if you would make me so.

Belle, tenés moy la promesse, *etc.*

My love, keep the promise, *etc.*

Et s'aucune dolour me blesse,
douls penser me confortera,

And if some sorrow wounds me
a sweet thought will bring me comfort,

et seul de voulour me donra
pour plus honnour ce de naresse.

and only your desire will give me
more honour than mockery.

Belle, tenés moy la promesse, *etc.*

My love, keep the promise, *etc.*

Belle, tenés moy has a directness and vitality not always found in late fifteenth-century French music, which sometimes suffered from over-sophistication. It differs from a normal *rondeau* in having two texts sung simultaneously. The lower is a simple folk-tune, *La triquotée*, which repeats itself for both A and B sections, as does the bass line. Thus only the *cantus* changes for the B section, being re-composed above the same lower parts. The use of folk material, the *quodlibet* feature and the maximum use of the minimum amount of music make *Belle, tenés moy* very much the poor man's *rondeau*, and would have made it something of a humorous piece in its day.

Instrumentation

It would be a shame not to enjoy the double text, so two voices (soprano and tenor) will be required on the top two lines, although *La triquotée* was so well known in its day that it would doubtless also have been played on instruments only. The bass line has an effective 'swing' to it due to the reiterated rhythm and simple intervals. An instrument with some vigour, like a rebec or crumhorn, would sound well and help to suggest the associations of the folk-song. Doubling instruments (recorder or flute), particularly on the top line, are a possibility, and would solve the problem of the melisma in bars 11 and 12 – the voice could either stop in the middle of bar 10 or continue the previous syllable. The very opening of the *cantus* could be played on an instrument alone since it is not easy to see how the words are intended to be underlayed.

Suggestions for interpretation

The ♩. rhythm is responsible for the 'swing', so it must not be too slow. The lively top line must, then, be very light and graceful. The 3/4 rhythm at the beginning of B must be emphasized as this is an enjoyable feature of its infrequent return. Some effort could be made to have a try at the original pronunciation of the French – see the bibliography for details.

A
Cantus
Tenor
Bassus
1. Bel -
2. Si__
3. Et__
La tri - quo - té - e est par ma-tin le - vé - e

- le, te - nés moy la pro-mes - se que
__________ j'ay du mal j'a - ray lé - es - se, tou-
__________ s'au - cu - ne do - lour me bles - se, douls
sa pris sa har - pe, au bois s'en est al - lé - e, la

10
vous me fies - tes pie - ca,
-tes les fois__ qu'il vous__ plai-ra.
pen - ser me__ con - for - te -ra,
tri - quo-ton, la tri - quo-ton, la bel - le tri - quo-té - e.

B

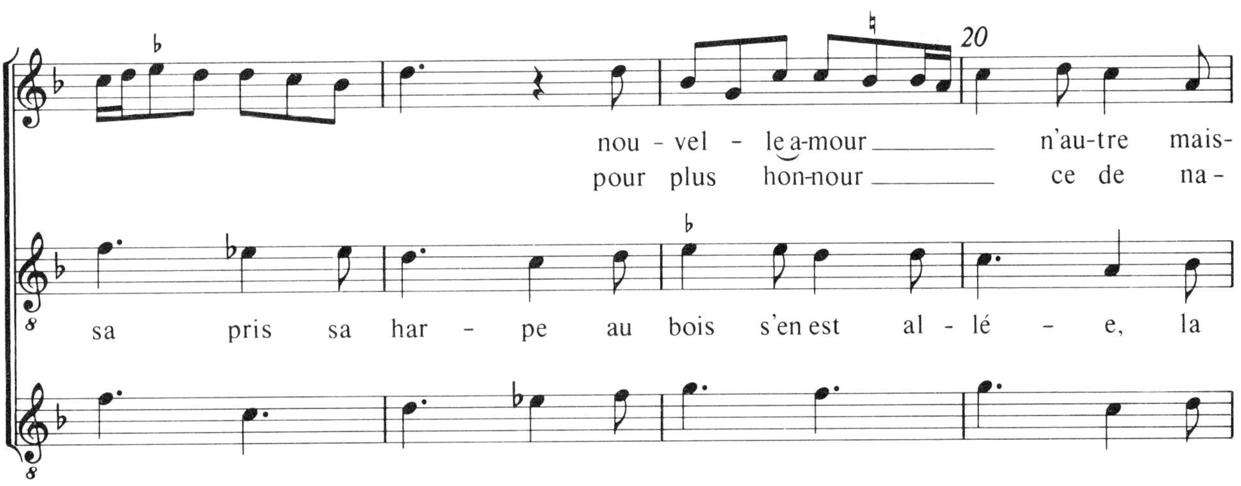

Rondeau A1 B1 A2 A1 A3 B2 A1 B1

14. *Las, je m'y plains* Claudin de Sermisy / Francesco da Milano

Las, je m'y plains, mauldicte soit fortune,	Alas, I lament my accursed fate,
quant pour aymer je n'ay que desplaisir.	in love I have only distress.
Venez, regretz, venez mon cueur saisir,	Come, regrets, come and seize my heart
et le monstrez a madame importune.	and show it to my troublesome mistress.

An extraordinary all-consuming fashion burst on the French musical scene in the 1520s: the four-part *chanson* blossomed overnight and remained in demand for the next forty years. Claudin was one of its chief masters and *Las, je m'y plains* is a typical example of his art. Perhaps the relatively simple style of the *chanson* was a reaction against the earlier over-sophistication of Burgundian court music; perhaps a rising middle class wished to ape court fashions but needed a simpler style in order to take part, for this is very much 'sing-a-part-yourself' music. But its success was assured by the support of the new young king, François I. His taste in fashion was coloured by his love of things Italian, which affected the clothes he wore and the food he ate. To be sure the suave French touch was not lost, but an Italianate flavour was unmistakable. The same can be said for the music, as the Paris *chanson* of the 1520s bears the noticeable influence of the Italian *frottola*. It is refined music wearing a popular guise. The essence of the style is vocal, and in this respect more thoroughgoing than its Italian counterpart, for the other three parts as well as the *cantus* are designed to be sung. This repertoire includes some of the finest vocal part-music ever written.

Instrumentation

A classic performance of this *chanson* would be vocal throughout. The ranges (SATB) are perfect, the phrase lengths equally so, and every line has its own delights. We must regard the voices as the prime instruments intended by Claudin. However, we know from other contemporary publications that many *chansons*, with only the minimum adaptation, were transformed into instrumental dances where a rich variety of instrumentation could rightly be employed. A quartet of viols, recorders or crumhorns would give the desired homogeneity of sound, but an especially French solution would be a quartet of flutes. Mixed instruments may also work satisfactorily, though care must be taken to maintain a natural balance between the parts. Finally, a lute intabulation is given here which is optional for ensemble performance, but is entirely satisfactory as a lute solo. It is intabulated by the Italian master Francesco da Milano (*fl.* 1520).

Suggestions for interpretation

There could be nothing more noble than to aim for the 'goulden meane' in the work. Neither too fast, nor too slow; neither too dramatic, nor too retiring; neither too loud, nor too soft – but just right.

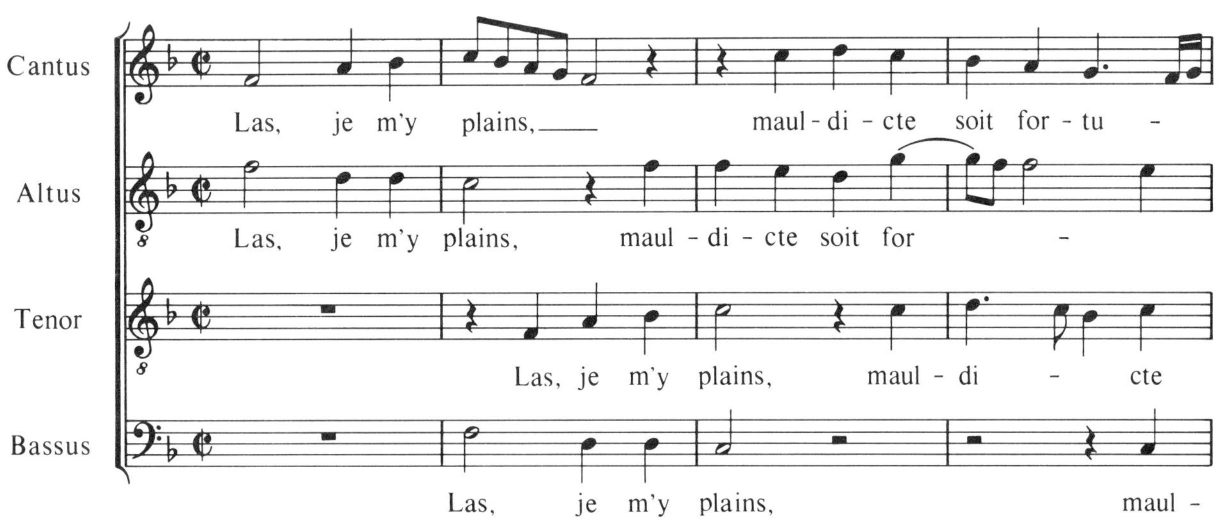
Cantus
Altus
Tenor
Bassus
Las, je m'y plains, maul - di - cte soit for - tu -
Las, je m'y plains, maul - di - cte soit for -
Las, je m'y plains, maul - di - cte
Las, je m'y plains, maul -

- - - ne, quant pour ay - mer
- tu - - ne, quant pour ay - mer, quant pour ay-
soit for - tu - ne, quant pour ay - mer, quant
- di - cte soit for - tu - ne, quant pour ay-mer

10
je n'ay que des-plai - sir. Ve - nez, re - gretz, ve -
-mer je n'ay que des-plai - sir. Ve - nez, re-gretz, ve - nez
pour aymer je n'ay que des-plai - sir. Ve - nez, re - gretz, ve -
je n'ay que des-plai - sir. Ve - nez, re-gretz, ve - nez, ve - nez mon

-nez mon cueur sai - sir, et le mon-strez a ma dame im-por -
mon cueur sai - sir, et le mon-strez a ma dame im-por -
-nez mon cueur sai - sir, et le mon-strez, et le mon-strez a ma
cueur sai - sir, et le mon-strez

20
-tu - - - ne, et le mon - strez
- - tu - - ne, et le mon - strez
dame im - por - tu - ne, et le mon - strez, et
a ma dame im - por - tu - ne, et

a ma dame im - por - tu - - - ne.
a ma dame im - por - tu - - ne.
le mon-strez a ma dame im - por - tu - ne.
le mon-strez a ma dame im - por - tu - ne.

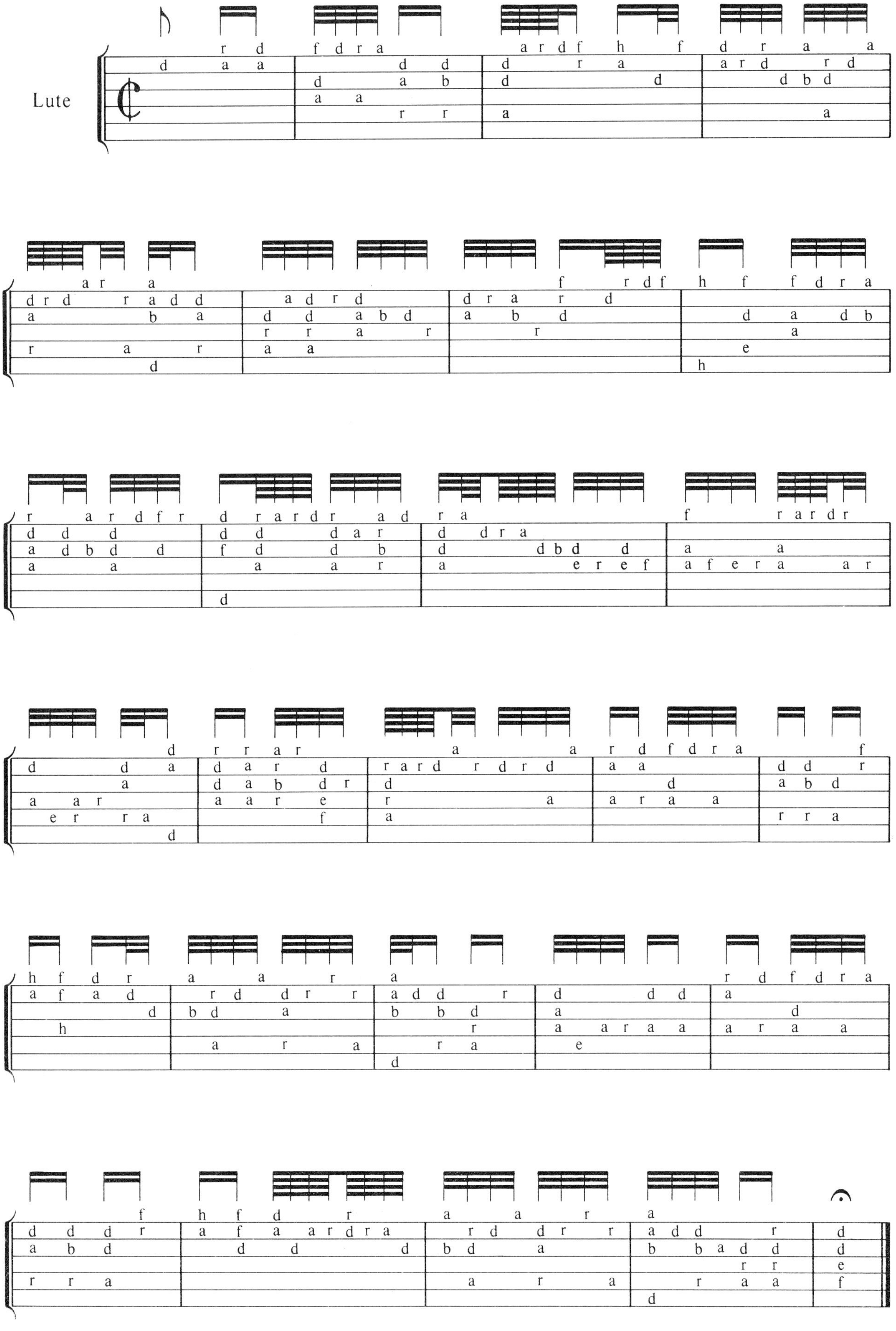

Lute

15. *Fière cruelle* Claude le Jeune

Fière cruelle en amour, fay moy ou vivre ou mourir. O miserable tourment, qu'ay du cruel jeu d'amour tel que ne scay le sentant bien recognoistre mon mal. Fière cruelle, *etc.*	Haughty, cruel in love, let me either live or die. Oh miserable torture is my cruel fate in the game of love, such that, feeling it, I cannot recognize that it is my misfortune. Haughty, cruel woman, *etc.*
Si je vivoy, je pourroy esperer au moins mourir, mais ou la vie n'est point, oncques la mort n'aborda, fière cruelle, *etc.*	If I were alive, at least I would be able to hope for death, but where there is no life death never comes, haughty, cruel woman, *etc.*
Lors trouverois de mes maux quelque defett' en la mort, mais ne vivant je languis pour ne mourant avoir pis. Fière cruelle, *etc.*	So I would seek in death some lessening of my misfortune, but I am languishing, not living, and a worse fate will befall me, not dying. Haughty, cruel woman, *etc.*

Emulation of classical Greek metre and 'sung-speech' is the inspiration behind Claude le Jeune's *chanson*. A considerable intellectual movement in France caused a break with the simple *chanson* style of Claudin de Sermisy and his generation. This movement centred on the poet Ronsard and was essentially concerned with elevating the French language to the level of respect accorded to Latin and Greek. It was primarily neoplatonic in its ideals, borrowing much from the Florentine court, and may be seen as another French movement inspired by Italian models. The Pléiade, as the group of poets was called, experimented with writing poetry in classical metre and in free speech rhythms. *Vers mesuré*, as it was dubbed, led to some very fine verse as well as to rather arid and fruitless experiments. Since it was believed that Greek poetry was intoned in a style midway between speaking and singing, contemporary composers were encouraged to experiment in setting these verses: the earliest public concerts of this material incorporated discussions of each work by the intelligentsia immediately after its performance. Only the most talented composers made real music out of these excessive restrictions, Claude le Jeune perhaps being the most successful.

Unusual bar lengths give a feeling of rhythmic freedom in *Fière cruelle*, a piece in which melodic, harmonic and rhythmic elements are wholly subservient to the language. Yet le Jeune's skill is such that the music remains powerful and memorable.

Instrumentation

The concern of the Pléiade for language was such that the use of instruments languished. A vocal performance with SATB is really the only satisfactory solution.

Suggestions for interpretation

Clear enunciation of the text is of paramount importance, and to this end the *tactus* must be treated with considerable freedom. *Rubato* is a vital ingredient so that emotive words, *'amour'*, *'mourir'*, *'misérable'*, etc., can have full impact. The vocal ensemble must move as one and intone the text much as the chorus in an ancient Greek tragedy might have done. Though the members of the Pléiade were no more familiar with Greek choruses than we are, the concept provided the inspiration.

Cantus
Altus
Tenor
Bassus
Fiè - re cru-elle en a-mour, fay moy ou vivre ou mou-rir.
Fiè - re cru-elle en a-mour, fay moy ou vivre ou mou-rir.
Fiè - re cru-elle en a-mour, fay moy ou vivre ou mou-rir.
Fiè - re cru-elle en a-mour, fay moy ou vi-vre ou mou-rir.
O mi-se-ra - ble tour - ment, qu'ay du cru-el jeu d'a-mour
O mi-se-ra - ble tour - ment, qu'ay du cru-el jeu d'a-mour
O mi-se-ra - ble tour - ment, qu'ay du cru-el jeu d'a-mour
O mi-se-ra - ble tour - ment, qu'ay du cru-el jeu d'a-mour
tel que ne scay le sen - tant bien re-co-gnois - tre mon mal.
tel que ne scay le sen - tant bien re-co-gnois - tre mon mal.
tel que ne scay le sen - tant bien re-co-gnois - tre mon mal.
tel que ne scay le sen - tant bien re-co-gnois - tre mon mal.

16. *Mignonne, allons voir si la rose* Anon.

Mignonne, allons voir si la rose qui ce matin avait desclose sa robe de pourpre au soleil a poinct perdu ceste vespree les plis de sa robe pourpree et son teinct au vostre pareil.	My sweet, let us go and see if the rose which this morning opened her crimson robe to the sun this evening still retains the folds of her red robe and her rosy complexion so like yours.
Las! voyez comme en peu d'espace, mignonne, elle a dessus la place hélas, ses beautez laissé choir! Ha, vrayment marastre est nature, puisqu'une telle fleur ne dure que du matin jusques au soir.	Alas, look, my sweet, how in so short a time she has shed her beauty, alas, on to the ground. Nature is truly a cruel mother if such a flower endures only from the morning till the evening.
Donc, si vous me croyez, mignonne, tandis que vostre age fleuronne, en sa plus verte nouveauté, cueillez, cueillez vostre jeunesse, comme à ceste fleur la vieillesse fera terner vostre beauté. Ronsard	Therefore, trust me, my sweet, while your life is still in full flower, still at the peak of its green freshness, pluck the flower of your youth, for, likewise, age will tarnish your beauty.

The artless simplicity of this song provides us with the other side of the coin from the sophistication of the *vers mesuré* of the previous work. Songs of this kind were called *voix-de-villes*, a word which was transformed, during ensuing centuries, into *vaudeville*. These were songs of supposedly rustic nature, pseudo-shepherd songs, as contrived in their way as were the experiments in classical metre. The famous poem by Ronsard is given an anonymous tune of real beauty, such as may have been on the lips of any rude shepherd in Arcardy.

Instrumentation

This love-plaint can be sung in any voice-range, provided that it is transposed to a key which utilizes the middle part of the voice. The F minor pitch was often used to signify a pastoral mood, but should not be taken as a fixed range. The accompaniment, if one is needed at all, should be simple. Perhaps a drone of tonic and fifth to a simple rhythm is enough. A gittern or lute would be ideal, though a bowed drone on a rebec or viol might be preferred.

Suggestions for interpretation

The simplest possible realization is desirable but it is not a folk-piece. It is pseudo-rustic and must carry a feeling of control and cultivation.

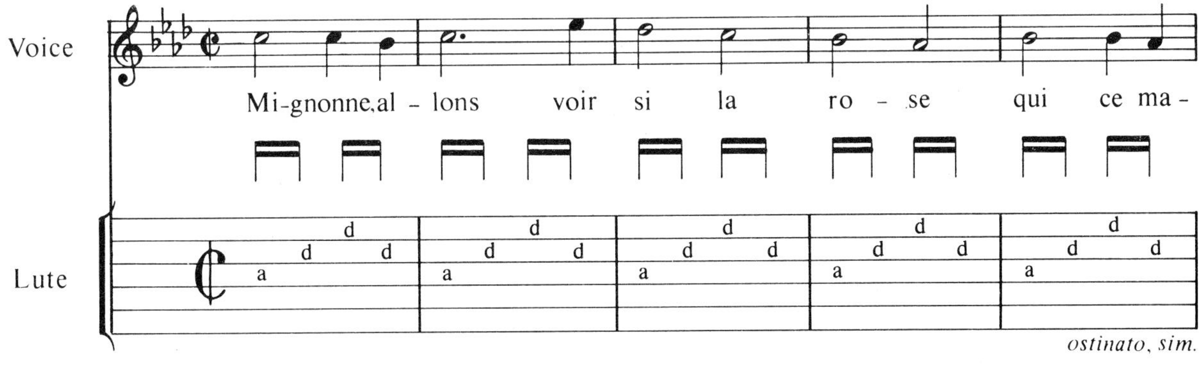

Las! voyez comme en peu d'espace,
mignonne, elle a dessus la place
hélas, ses beautez laissé choir!
Ha, vrayment marastre est nature,
puisqu'une telle fleur ne dure
que du matin jusques au soir.

Donce, si vous me croyez, mignonne,
tandis que vostre age fleuronne,
en sa plus verte nouveauté,
cueillez, cueillez vostre jeunesse,
comme à ceste fleur la vieillesse
fera terner vostre beauté.

17. *Christ der ist erstanden* Anon./Judenkunig

Christ der ist erstanden	Christ is arisen
von des todesbanden,	from the bonds of death,
des sollen wir alle fro sein.	therefore we should all be joyful.
Alleluja.	Alleluia.

This timeless, haunting tune could only come from Germany and the fact that it was known in the fifteenth century shows that chorale-like tunes preceded the Protestant movement. We must assume a national predilection for such melodic and rhythmic simplicity that goes deeper than religious controversy. It appears to have been a Germanic trait also to place the tune in the *tenor* rather than the *cantus*, which was common practice elsewhere. This three-part setting, from the *Glogauer Liederbuch* compiled between 1460 and 1480, is one of the earliest sources of the tune, although the complex outer parts suggest that the melody was already well known and would be easily recognized. The lute version, printed by Hans Judenkunig in 1523, was probably also written in the fifteenth century. The plangent, dying sound of the lute provides a perfect instrumental realization of this melody.

Instrumentation

A voice could double the tune in the lute solo if required: the naturalness of the tune is such that as soon as one knows it one wishes to join in. Certainly a voice singing the middle part of the three-part setting is preferable, with perhaps a recorder on the *cantus* and a rebec on the *bassus* (if indeed a '*grossgeigen*' ever played so low!). Almost any instruments with the appropriate ranges could play these parts, which seem to be of a genuinely instrumental character. An all-instrumental performance is really quite appropriate too. This repertoire provides a very good source of wind-band music but is equally satisfying for strings, rebecs, *vielles* and lutes (preferably plucked with a quill).

Suggestions for interpretation

The smooth, *legato* tune should naturally contrast with the rhythmically incisive outer parts. The delight is in the opposite characters inter-playing; sacred and secular in harmony as it were. The bare two-part writing in the lute solo suggests that the two notes should not be 'broken' or 'rolled' but played simultaneously. To play the lute part on a guitar, see the note on piece number 9.

Cantus
Tenor
Christ der ist er - stan - - den
Bassus
von des to - des ban - - den, des
sol - len wir al - le fro sein. Al -
- - le - - lu - ja.
Lute in A

18. *Elslein, liebstes Elselein* Anon.

Elslein, liebstes Elselein, wie gern waer ich bei dir. So sein zwei tiefe wasser wol zwischen dir und mir.	Elsie, dearest little Elsie, how I wish I were with you. But two deep seas lie between you and me.
Das bringt mir grosse schmerzen, herzallerliebster gsell! Red'ich von ganzem herzen habs fuer gros ungefaell.	That brings me great pain, my dearest sweetheart! This I say from my full heart: I think it is a great misfortune.
Hoff, zeit werd es wol enden, hoff, glueck werd kommen drein, sich in alls guts verwenden, herzliebstes Elselein.	I hope that in time it may end, I hope that happiness may come, and everything may turn out for the best, my dearest little Elsie.

Romantic love songs with simple, catchy melodies have a long history in Germany. So that we might indulge our romantic tendencies fully in this gentle parting song, several original sources have been brought together in a composite arrangement.

Instrumentation

The recommended instrumentation for this particular arrangement is as follows:

Verse 1: tenor voice and lute (first stanza)
Verse 2: two rebecs
Verse 3: tenor voice and lute (second stanza)
Verse 4: two lutes
Verse 5: tenor voice, two lutes, two rebecs (third stanza)

This is undoubtedly *not* a method of performance that can claim to be authentic, though it is extremely effective. A free use of near-folk music is quite legitimate in any age of course and its success dictates its veracity. With the raw materials presented here, several other solutions can be found. The two-part version is especially effective when played on two flutes or recorders, for example.

Suggestions for interpretation

A direct approach is intrinsic to the style and although the piece has a strong romantic flavour it must not be too slow, nor should the cadences be too drawn out by *rubato*. A folksy simpleness will serve best.

A

1. Els - lein, lieb - stes El - se-lein, wie gern waer ich bei
3. Das bringt mir gros - se schmerz - en, herz - all - er-lieb - ster

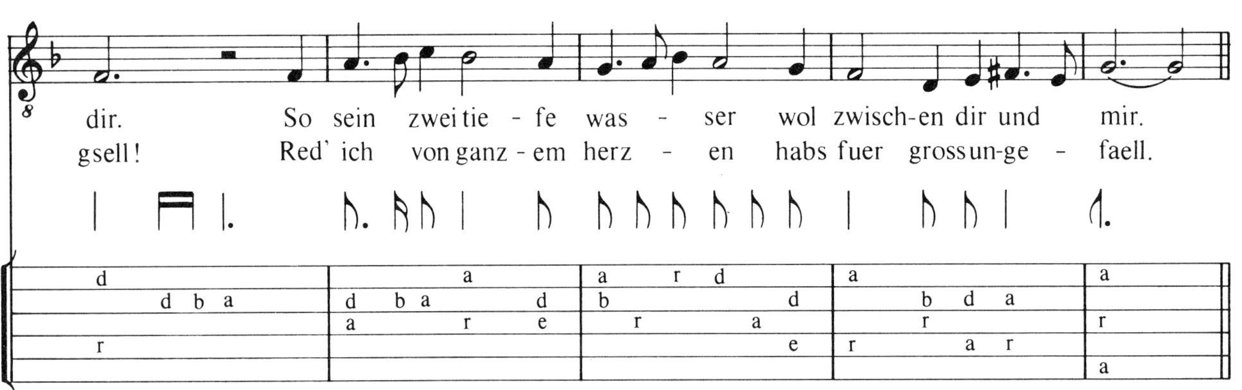
dir. So sein zwei tie - fe was - ser wol zwisch-en dir und mir.
gsell! Red' ich von ganz - em herz - en habs fuer gross un-ge - faell.

B verses 2 and 4

C

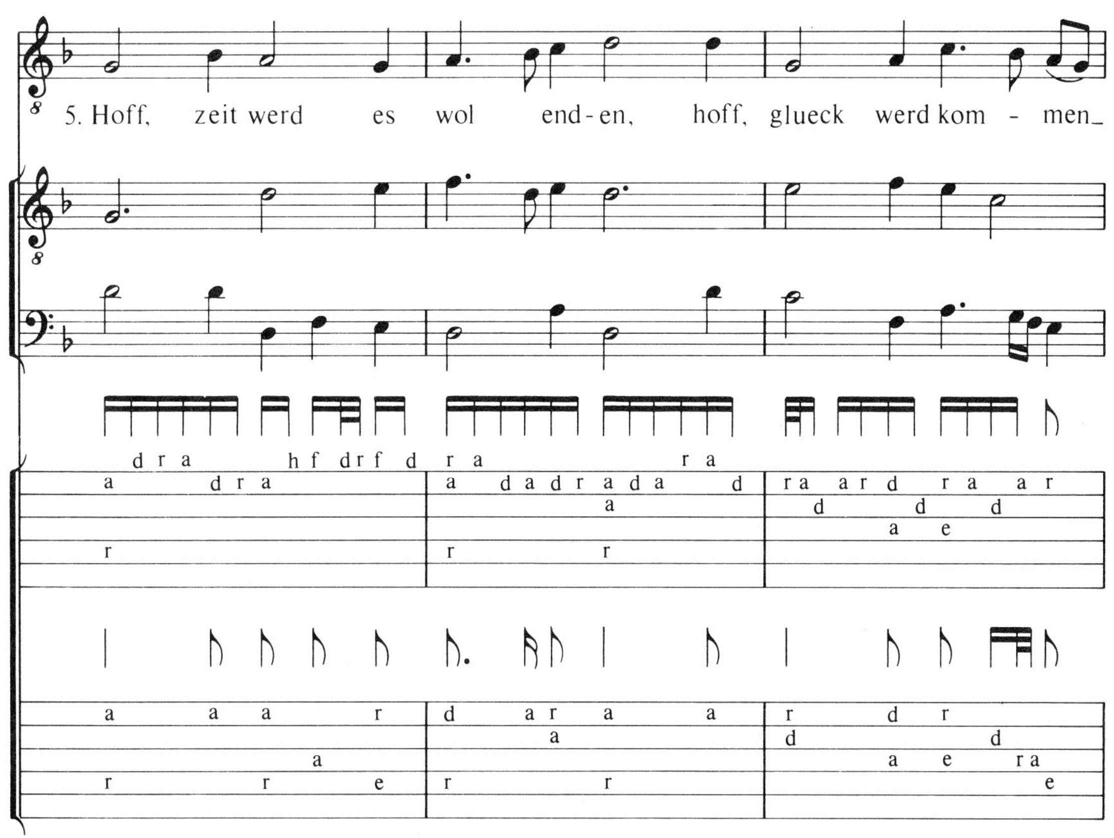
5. Hoff, zeit werd es wol end-en, hoff, glueck werd kom - men_

drein, sich in allsguts ver-wend - en, herz-lieb-stes El-se - lein.

19. *Vitrum nostrum gloriosum* Georg Forster

Vitrum nostrum gloriosum,	Our glorious glass
eo gratissimum,	most welcome to the drinker,
o vitrum.	oh glass:
Levate!	raise it!
Fac, fac, bibe totum extra,	Go on, go on, drink it all up,
ut nihil maneat intra.	so that nothing be left within;
Depone!	put it down!
Hoc est in visceribus meis.	Now it's in my insides.
Prosequamur laude!	Let us honour it with praise!

Chorale tunes and romantic love songs traditionally belong to Germany; so do boisterous drinking songs. *Vitrum nostrum gloriosum* is an especially interesting kind of song in praise of wine since it also takes a rise out of the pomp and ritual of 'popery'. The song is interspersed with mock-Gregorian chant sung with sacrilegious words in a drunken, monkish tone, no doubt in mockery of a priest. Forster published a complete collection of such drinking songs, especially written for university-student consumption. They were good fun and well received, but they also had a deliberate political purpose and were intended to inculcate derision of Catholicism in the young.

Instrumentation

Drinking songs must of course be sung, and sung in a suitably forthright and lusty manner. There is little call for subtlety here. We do not know if instruments supported the voices but we can presume that if anything was to hand it would be played. The lute part is a makeshift of the three lower parts and is a conjecture of what a handy lutenist might have played.

Suggestions for interpretation

Interpretation is too fine a word in this context, 'ham-up' might be closer. The chant sections should sound monkish *and* boozy at the same time. The interval of the fifth at the beginning of the second chant could sound very drunken by sliding up to the D. Such a 'basic' song needs good intonation in the four-part sections – true fifths will sound very well.

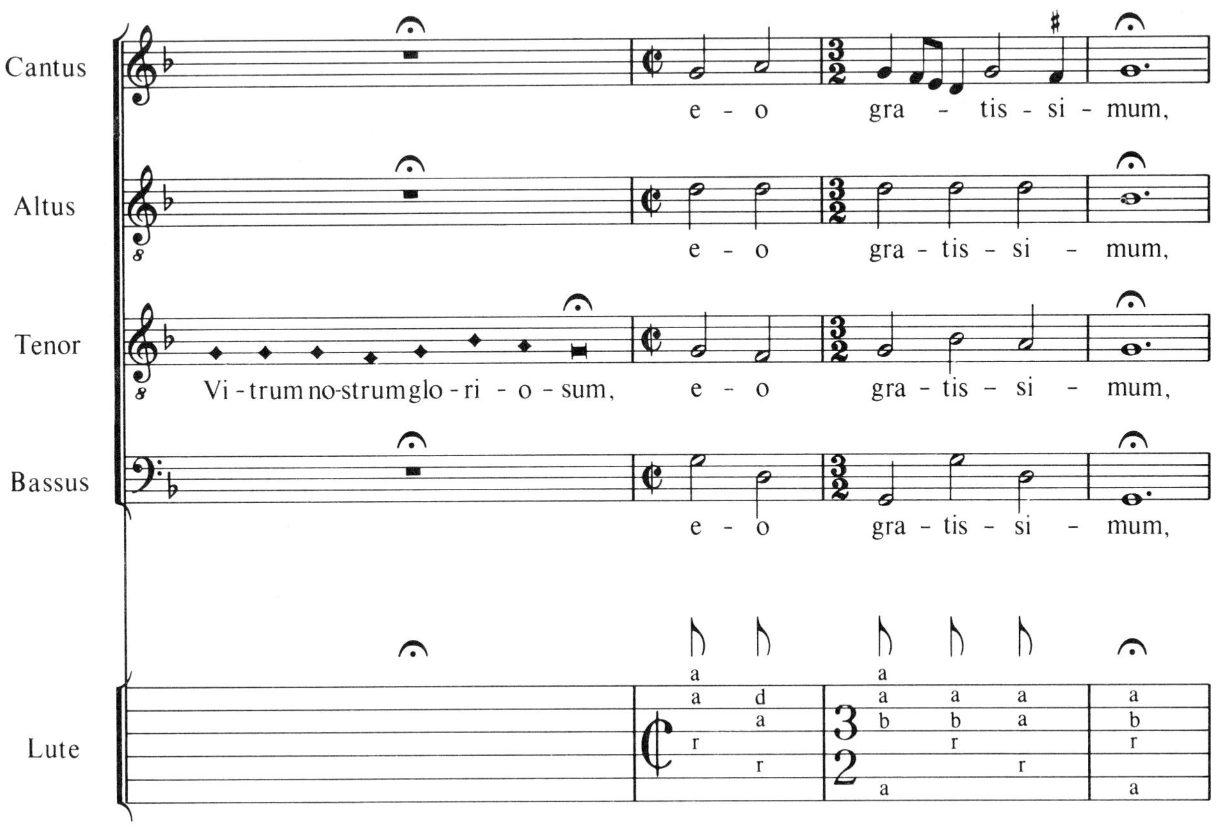
Cantus
e - o gra - tis - si - mum,
Altus
e - o gra - tis - si - mum,
Tenor
Vi - trum no-strum glo - ri - o - sum, e - o gra - tis - si - mum,
Bassus
e - o gra - tis - si - mum,
Lute

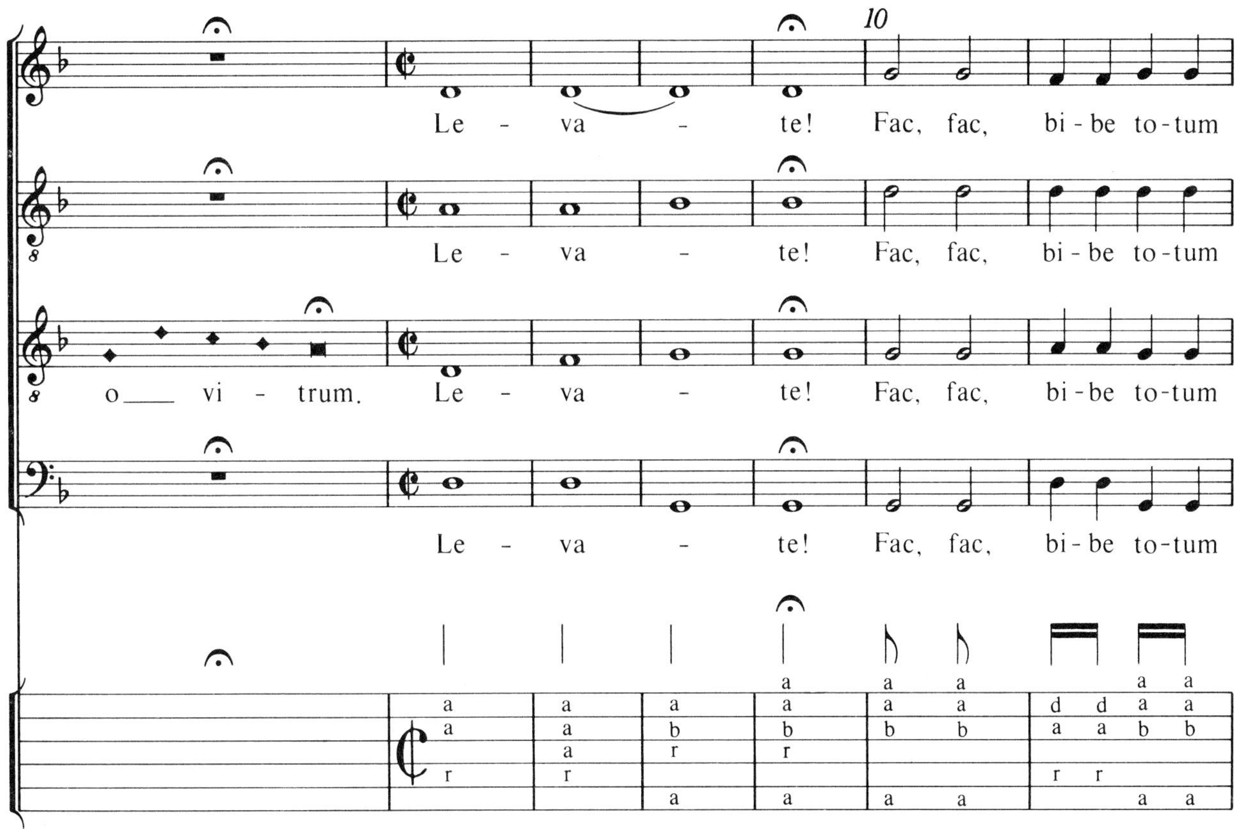
Le - va - te! Fac, fac, bi - be to - tum
Le - va - te! Fac, fac, bi - be to - tum
o vi - trum. Le - va - te! Fac, fac, bi - be to - tum
Le - va - te! Fac, fac, bi - be to - tum

ex - tra, ut ni - hil ma - ne-at in - tra, fac, bi - be to - tum
ex - tra, ut ni - hil ma - ne-at in - tra, fac, bi - be to - tum
ex - tra, ut ni - hil ma - ne-at in - tra, fac, bi - be to - tum
ex - tra, ut ni - hil ma - ne-at in - tra, fac, bi - be to - tum

20
ex - tra, ut ni - hil ma - ne-at in - tra, De - po - ne!
ex - tra, ut ni - hil ma - ne-at in - tra, De - po - ne!
ex - tra, ut ni - hil ma - ne-at in - tra, De - po - ne!
ex - tra, ut ni - hil ma - ne-at in - tra, De - po - ne!

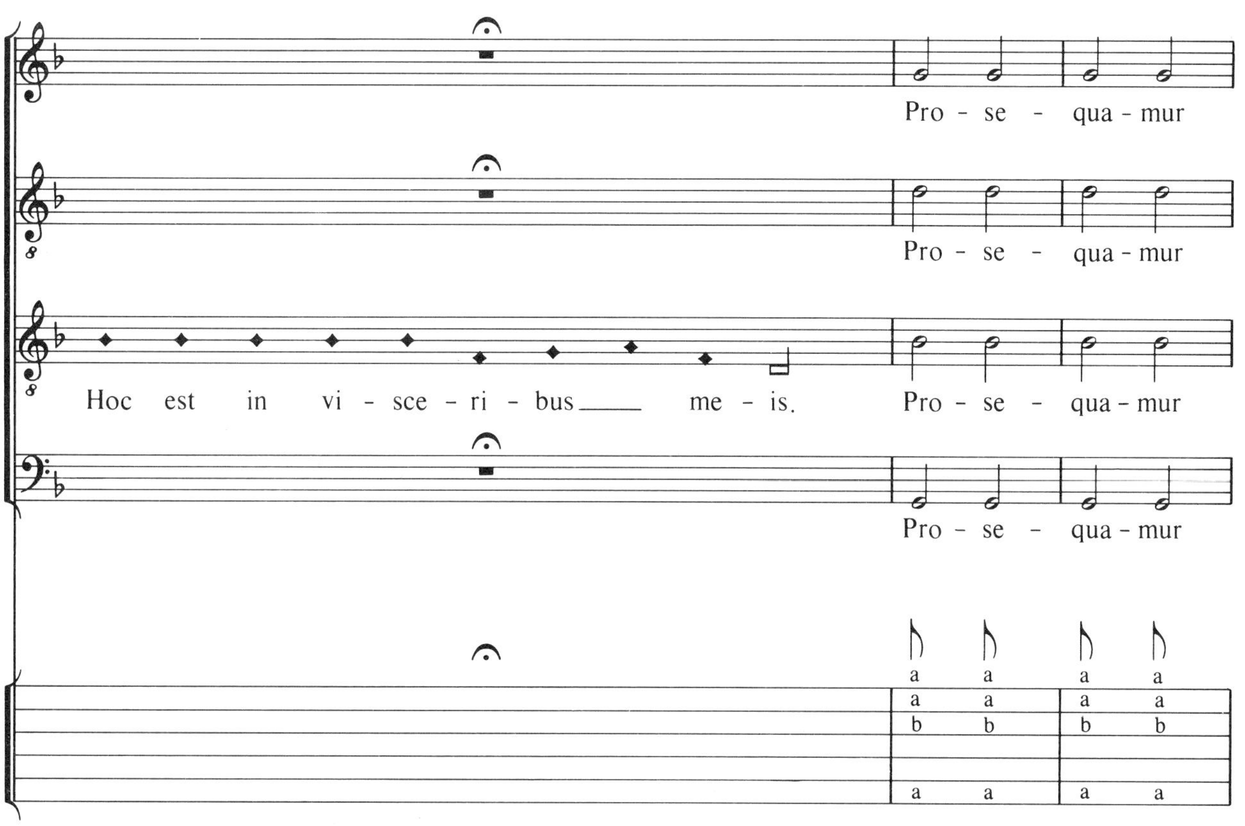
Pro - se - qua - mur
Pro - se - qua - mur
Hoc est in vi - sce - ri - bus me - is. Pro - se - qua - mur
Pro - se - qua - mur

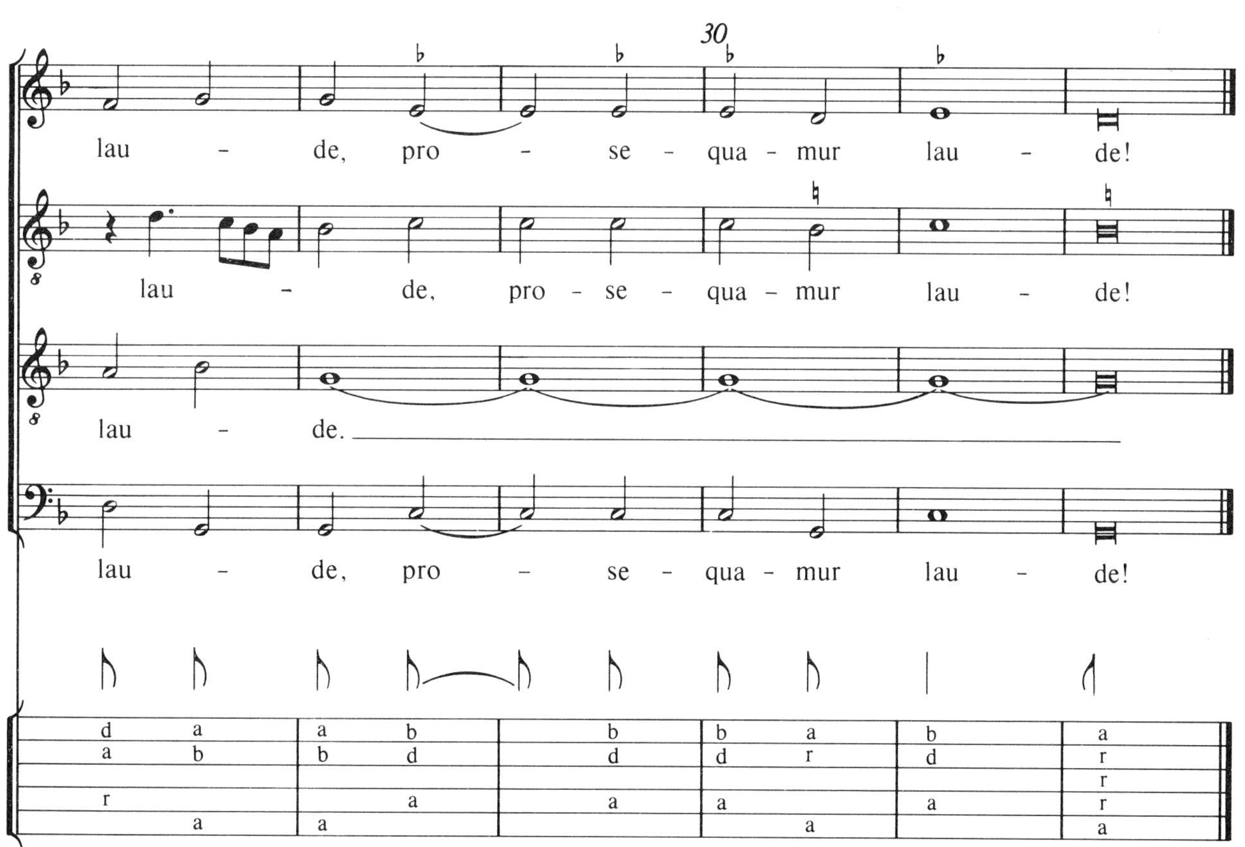
30
lau - de, pro - se - qua - mur lau - de!
lau - de, pro - se - qua - mur lau - de!
lau - de.
lau - de, pro - se - qua - mur lau - de!

20. *La Spagna* Francisco de la Torre

The *basse danse* was the most widespread dance of fifteenth-century Europe, its steps as formal and repetitive as the poetry and music of the *rondeau*. The music for the *basse danse* was less rigorous, for the tradition of accompanying dance was largely oral and improvisatory. We can imagine groups of three or so musicians 'jamming' together providing jazzy divisions whilst the nobility danced their serene steps. The band must have known the repertoire backwards, for almost no contemporary music settings survive. There were many famous tunes used to accompany the *basse danse*, some appropriated from the current *chanson* repertoire, and some, like *La Spagna*, developed especially for dancing. We do not know if *La Spagna* refers to Spain as the country of origin, but it makes particular sense in this context as Francisco de la Torre was one of the major composers at the court of Ferdinand and Isabella. He was not the composer of the tune, for that belongs to a long oral tradition, but he did compose the two outer parts, the florid *cantus* or treble (*tipla* in Spanish) and the supporting *bassus*. The 'tenor' *La Spagna* normally appears in the *tenor* part, as one would expect, but not invariably so – sometimes it becomes the *bassus* or, more rarely, the *cantus*. Of all the *basse danse* 'tenors', *La Spagna* seems to have been, for quite inexplicable reasons, far and away the most popular. Well over a hundred instrumental settings survive, many composed well after a *basse danse* would ever have been performed. It may be that none of the surviving settings were intended for actual dance use, but were composed 'fantasias' on the 'tenor' or *cantus firmus*. Francisco's version is a classic of its kind. The vigorous top line is of a very improvisatory nature and pursues its way relentlessly to the final cadence.

Instrumentation

Most illustrations of dance-bands of the fifteenth century show either a single musician playing both pipe and tabor (our version is clearly not for him), or a wind-band of three players with various combinations of shawms and sackbutts. An ideal loud consort for this piece would be a shawm on the *cantus* line, with two sackbutts on the *tenor* and *bassus*. If a more domestic realization is preferred, try a plectrum-played lute on the top with two rebecs or viols below. The permutations of possibilities with this repertoire are endless, and every player should be given an opportunity to attempt the virtuoso part, which conveys vividly the vitality of the period.

Suggestions for interpretation

The *tenor* and *bassus* should be firm and sustained with breath marks agreed between the two parts. Deciding where these should be is more difficult: one is tempted to say 'wherever you really need to' for it is impossible to establish sounder criteria. At least if the two parts breathe together it helps to give coherence. The independent *cantus* must make the most of the swinging syncopations, so too slow a speed should be avoided. Against the lively treble, especially effective cross-rhythms can be made in the lower parts across bars 5–6, 11–12, 30–31, 33–34 and 35–36, all shown as dotted bar-lines.

Cantus
Tenor
Bassus
10

20
30

21. *Adoramos te, Señor* Francisco de la Torre

Adoramos te, Señor, Dios y hombre Jhesu Cristo, en el sacramento visto, universal redentor.	We worship thee, Lord, Jesus Christ, God and Man, through Holy Communion, our universal Redeemer.
Adoramos te vitoria de la santa vera cruz, que nos dejas te en memoria y el cuerdo lleno de luz.	We worship thy victory over the agony of the Cross, which thou gavest us in remembrance of thee, filling our souls with light.
Criatura y criador, dios y hombre Jhesu Cristo, en el sacramento visto, adoramos te, Señor.	Jesus Christ, child and Creator, God and man, we worship thee, Lord, in Holy Communion.

Catholicism so pervaded the music-making of the Spanish court under Ferdinand and Isabella that secular works and secular forms were made vehicles for religious expression. The *cancion* form of the *villancico* (Spain's version of the *frottola* of the north-Italian courts) was decidedly secular in inspiration but was frequently put to religious use. This fine *villancico* by Francisco has a serene and contemplative atmosphere far removed from some racy works which might appear under the same form-name. Simplicity is the essence of his technique here, where the setting of the words is monosyllabic and the accompaniment is homophonic. All the more telling therefore are the occasional melismas (bars 13–15, 26–27, etc.) and harmonic suspensions. This is the timeless beauty of a devout and proud age.

Instrumentation

Many Arabic instruments came to Europe via Spain as legacies of its time of Moorish rule (711–1492). So it seems reasonable to assume, in absence of evidence to the contrary, that the viol which first became popular in Spain in the late fifteenth century was one of them. The tranquillity of *Adoramos te* is probably best realized by a consort of three viols – their dark colour and vocal qualities blend so well with the sung line, which here suits the tenor range. But Spain is also the home of exotic instruments, and one can imagine buzzing wind instruments (crumhorns, *rauschpfeifen*, etc.) providing an exciting accompaniment. In this case the singer would have to declaim with fervency, rather than quietly contemplate, his love for his Saviour.

Suggestions for interpretation

The phrasing of the instruments must be entirely in accord with the voice, whose breath-points are self-explanatory. We may debate the relationship of the triple proportion at bar 18 – perhaps the best solution is to keep the minim constant.

Cantus
Altus
Tenor
Bassus
1. A - do - ra - mos te, Se - ñor,
4. Cri - a - tu - ra y cri - a - dor,
Dios y

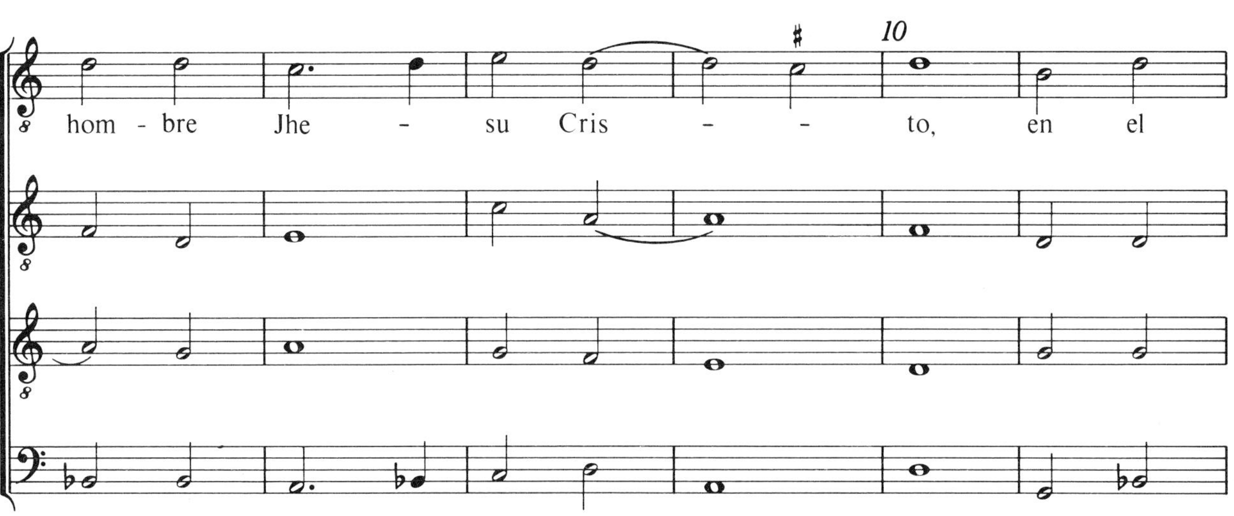
10
hom - bre Jhe - su Cris - - to, en el

sac - ra - men - - - to vis - to,

1
4
Fine
u - ni - ver - sal re - den - tor.
a - do - ra - mos te, Se - ñor.

2. A - do - ra - mos te vi - to - - ria
3. que nos de - jas te en me - mo - - ria

D.C. al Fine
de la san - ta ve - ra cruz,
y el cuer - do lle - no de luz.

22. *I love, loved* Robert Fayrfax

I love, loved, and loved wolde I be
in steadfast fayth and trouth with assurance;
then bownden were I such on faythfully to love,
thowe I do fere to trace that daunce,
lest that mysaventure myzt fall be chaunce;
yet will I me trust to fortune applye;
hough that evyr it will happ I wote nere I.
I love, loved, *etc.*

There is an indefinable Englishness about the secular work of the early Tudor composers such as Fayrfax, Cornyshe and the rest. Compared to contemporary Flemish, Italian and French music it has certain conservative, late-medieval features, but there is a rich vein of national individuality which could have flowered into a powerful Renaissance of England's own. Vitality and humour come across, much as in the verse of the first Poet Laureate, John Skelton, whose vituperative wit gave a new impetus to the English language. The composers were capable of (and gave) the same contributions to music – more's the pity therefore that religious, political and social upheavals completely prevented the next generation from realizing the implications of this rich native genius. The style of Fayrfax became, sadly, a musical backwater. But the rediscovery is well worthwhile. He commonly begins a new couplet in relatively slow notes and rather homophonically. The texture breaks, the parts scatter and become independent so that by the first cadence the texture is quite fragmented. The parts gather and break again like the surf breaking on the ceaseless tide. All parts frequently conclude, at the last syllable of a couplet, with an energetic and lengthy melisma in each line. We assume that the singers vocalize, using the vowel sound of the last syllable to carry them through the melisma. A whole world, revealing what English Renaissance music might have been like, is waiting to be discovered here.

Instrumentation

Despite the rugged contours of the lines and the jagged rhythms, this is essentially vocal music. The standard of singing at the courts of the two Henrys was probably very high indeed, and the physically demanding music (sacred and secular) clearly shows the agility expected of professional singers. The question of how much use should be made of instruments in this repertoire is a very vexing one. The independent character of each line suggests that doubling voices with instruments will only obscure the clarity of the parts. On the other hand, rhythmic precision might be increased by doubling with an instrument like the lute, which often has the effect of 'etching out' a part. Without more historical evidence, we can only experiment with voice and instrument combinations, accepting and discarding through our own aural judgement and expanding experience. One mistake which is often made is to mix *hauts* and *bas* (loud and soft) instruments, a practice neither having historic foundation, nor aural satisfaction, for some part must be obscured as another is forced into prominence. This music of the early Tudor court has vigour and vitality but also very great refinement. *Bas* instruments such as the lute, harp, flute, viol or *vielle* are the only appropriate instruments for such esoteric chamber music.

Suggestions for interpretation

The pronunciation of the language has changed almost beyond recognition, so the task of reconstructing a dialect that Fayrfax would have recognized as familiar is a daunting one. Experts disagree of course, and we are still awaiting the layman's guide to early Tudor pronunciation; meanwhile, speaking the words with as much love and vigour as we would normally expect of an Italian should help to shake off any indifference to exciting word-patterns. Most of the phrases begin broad and smooth and move to a pointillist agitation – we should encourage that tendency in approaching the phrasing. The faster the rhythmic values, the lighter the notes should be, so that the final notes of a long melisma feel rhythmic but airy. Careful attention to intonation is important – so many bare intervals and unisons can quickly sound dire. An editorial *da capo al fine* is marked to give a stronger final cadence. This can of course be completely ignored, for the manuscript gives no such indication.

Cantus
Tenor
Bassus
I love, lov - ed, and lov - ed wolde I be
I love, lov - ed, and lov - ed wolde I be
I love, lov - ed, and lov - ed wolde I be
in sted-fast fayth and trouth with as - su-rance;
in sted-fast fayth and trouth with as - su - rance;
in sted-fast fayth and trouth with as - su-rance;
10
then bownd-en were
then
then bownd-en were
I such on faythful - ly to love, thowe I do fere to trace that
bownd-en were I such on faythful-ly to love, thowe I do fere to trace that
I such on faythful - ly to love, thowe I do fere to trace that

Fine
daunce,
daunce,
daunce,
lest that mys - a - ven - ture myzt fall be chaunce; yet will I me
lest that mys - a - ven - ture myzt fall be chaunce; yet will I me
lest that mys - a - ven - ture myzt fall be chaunce; yet will I me
trust to for - tune ap-plye; how that ev - yr it will hap I wote nere I.
trust to for - tune ap-plye; how that ev - yr it will hap I wote nere I.
trust to for - tune ap-plye; how that ev - yr it will hap I wote nere I.
D.C. al Fine

23. *Blame not my lute* Anon.

Blame not my lute for he must sownde
of thes or that as liketh me;
for lake of wytt the lutte is bownde
to gyve suche tunes as plesithe me:
tho my songes be sume what strange,
and spekes suche wordes as toche they change,
blame no my lutte.

My lutte and strynges may not deny,
but as I strike they must obay;
brake not them then so wrongfully,
but wryeke they selff some wyser way
and tho the songes whiche I endighte
do qwytt thy change with rightful spight,
blame not my lute.

Farwell, unknowne, for tho thow brake
my strynges in spight with gratt desdayn,
yet have I fownde owtt for thy sake
strings for to strynge my lute agayne;
and yf perchance this folysh rymyme
do make the blushe at any tyme,
blame nott my lute.

Sir Thomas Wyatt

Reconstructing the missing link in secular music between Robert Fayrfax and William Byrd is a difficult but rewarding task, though the results provide only a sketch. This little lute-song, one of Sir Thomas Wyatt's best-known poems, gives an idea of the style of singing to the lute in the generation before Dowland and the *English Ayre* series of publications. Many of Wyatt's poems were intended to be sung, though almost no contemporary musical settings have survived. The likelihood is that he had a certain body of existing tunes in mind which provided convenient pegs on which to hang his lyrics – as in *Blame not my lute*. This particular tune is Italian. We do not know if Wyatt found it himself whilst in Italy, or whether he took it from a manuscript collection of Italian dances presented to Henry VIII, but the resulting combination of words and music is wholly delightful. Further possible settings of his lyrics from this and similar sources remain to be researched. In Italy the tune (and harmonic sequence) was known as *La Gamba* or *La Caracossa*.

Instrumentation

The most likely and direct instrumentation is voice and lute, with the voice being equally successful at soprano or tenor range. The key should be adjusted to suit the particular voice. Other accompaniments are possible, and no doubt any one of the combinations found in Italian dance music can be used to accompany the song: lute duet and trio, three-part and four-part ensemble, keyboard, etc., etc. Three viols and lute would provide an appropriate sonority.

Suggestions for interpretation

The original poem has six stanzas, and the others can be included as desired (see p. 129 of *Sir Thomas Wyatt, The Complete Poems* – Penguin English Poets). Wyatt's language is rich and rhythmic and would benefit immensely from an effort to use an early pronunciation. An effect of sung-speech should be aimed for. Ornaments in both parts arising directly from the sense of the words will help give momentum, especially if many stanzas are performed. As a general guide the early verses should be fairly simple with more ornamentation as the story unfolds.

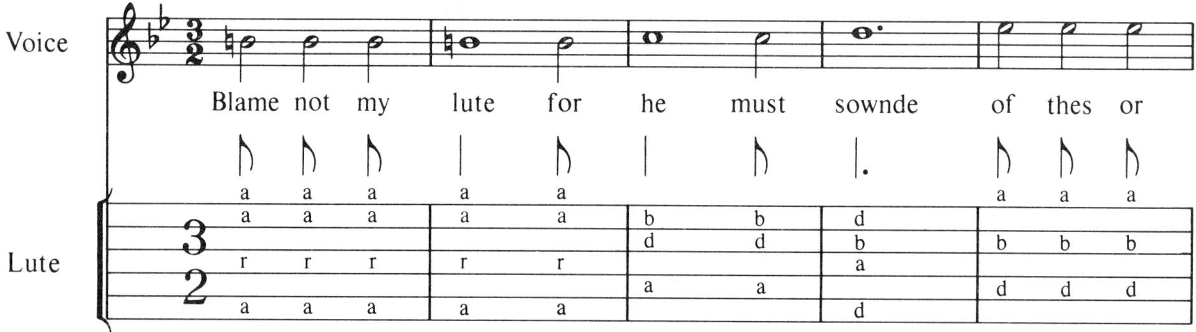

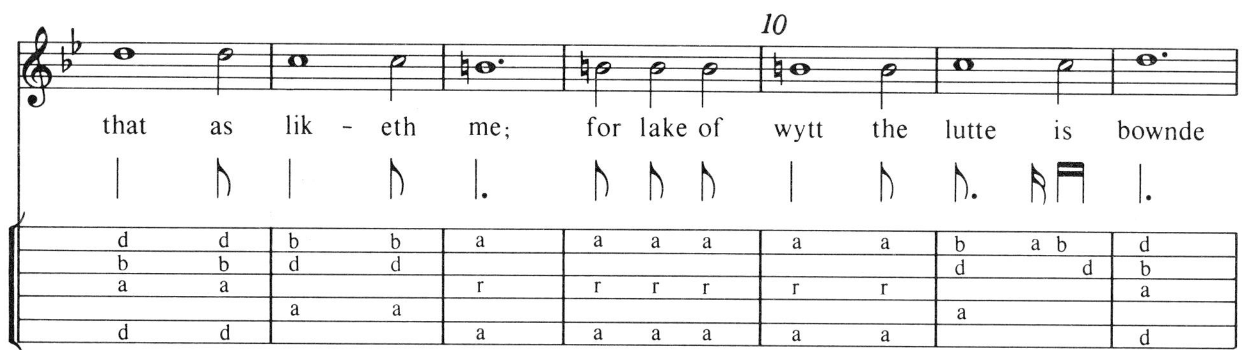

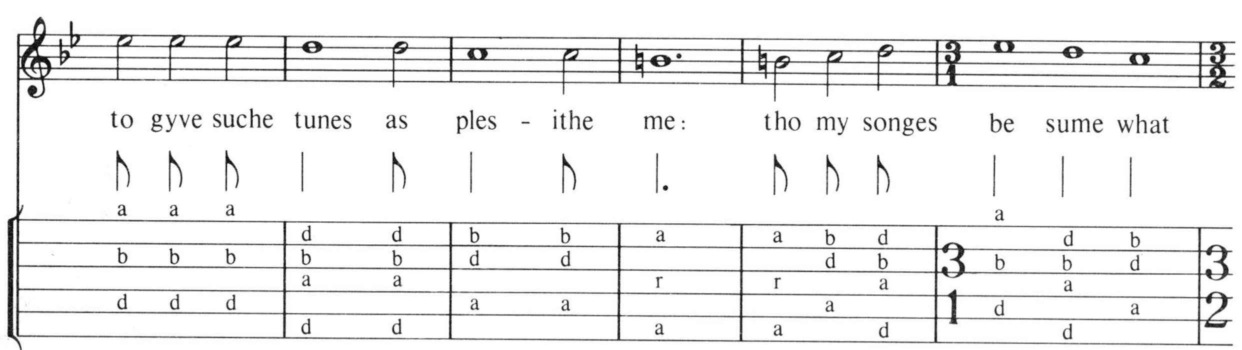

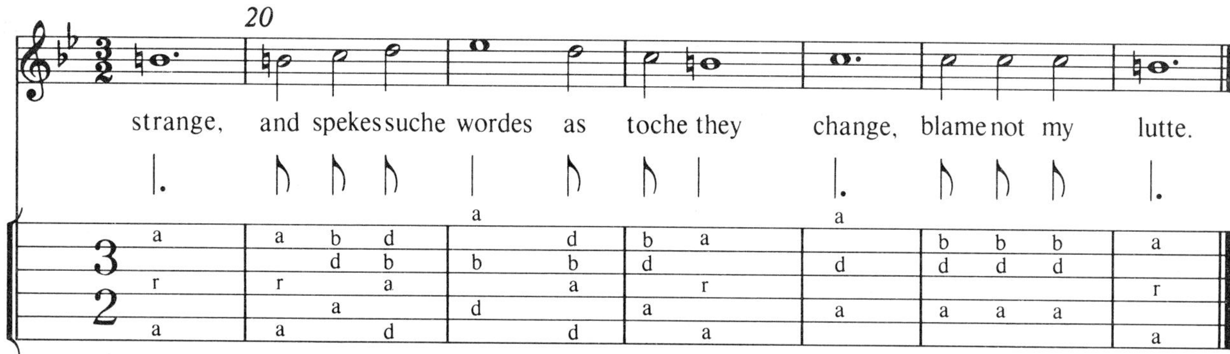

My lutte and strynges may not deny,
but as I strike they must obay;
brake not then so wrongfully,
but wryeke they selff some wyser way
and tho the songes whiche I endighte
do qwytt thy change with rightful spight,
blame not my lute.

Farwell, unknowne, for tho thow brake
my strynges in spight with gratt desdayn,
yet have I fownde owtt for thy sake
strings for to strynge my lute agayne;
and yf perchance this folysh rymyme
do make the blushe at any tyme,
blame nott my lute.

Cantus
Altus
Tenor
Bassus

24. *Where griping griefs* Anon.

Where griping griefs the heart would wound,
and doleful dumps the mind oppress,
there music with her silver sound
with speed is wont to send redress;
of troubled minds in every sore,
sweet music hath a salve in store.

In joy it makes our mirth abound,
in woe it cheers our heavy sprites,
bestrawghted heads relief hath found,
by musickes pleasant sweet delights;
our senses all, what shall I say more,
are subject unto musickes lore.

Richard Edwards

This brief encomium or 'ditty of Musicke's praise' is a favourite of many poetry anthologies, though the equally charming anonymous music setting is less well known, outside specialist circles. It is an appropriate union of music and poetry, and the intervals in the tune at bars 6 and 18 make it particularly distinctive. The only surviving version of this piece is arranged for solo cittern, so the present realization is edited from that. The problem of *ficta* (which could have been troublesome in a piece of this kind) is resolved by the precise notation of the tablature which leaves no doubt as to the raising and flattening of notes.

Instrumentation

A voice (at either octave) could be accompanied by any combination of *bas* instruments, with a preference for that most English of ensembles, the viol consort song (three or four viols and voice, preferably a 'meane' or 'treble'). If a tenor voice is used, then his line may be doubled by a tenor recorder at the higher octave, which, with three viols and a lute, makes a most euphonious combination, quite in accord with the ditty.

Suggestions for interpretation

Natural word-accent often goes against the implied bar accent – always follow the language. The opening of every phrase can, for example, be thought of as if it were a 3/2 bar with a crotchet anacrusis. The accent then falls well for the words. With so much talk of music, the poem affords many opportunities for ornaments (divisions rather than graces), to be regarded as word-painting. 'Abound' for instance begs for some quaver movement, whilst 'pleasant sweet delights' calls for some acknowledgement. In this homophonic style phrasing must be precise.

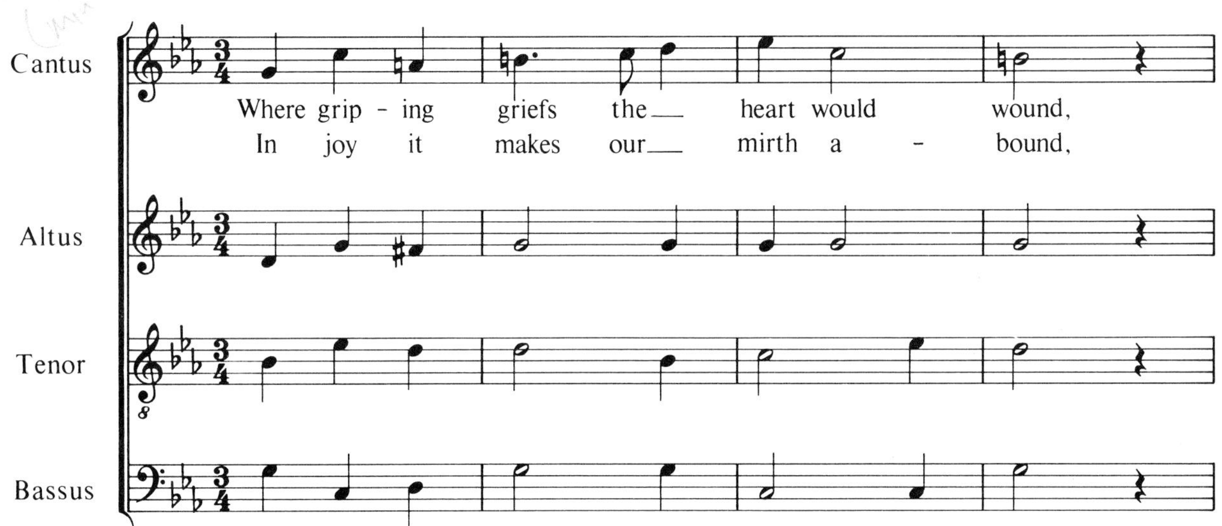
Cantus
Altus
Tenor
Bassus
Where grip - ing griefs the heart would wound,
In joy it makes our mirth a - bound,

and dole - ful dumps the mind op - ress,
in woe it cheers our hea - vy sprites,

10
there mu - sic with her sil - ver sound
be strawght - ed heads re - lief hath found,

with speed is wont to send re - dress:
by mu - sickes pleas - ant sweet de - lights;

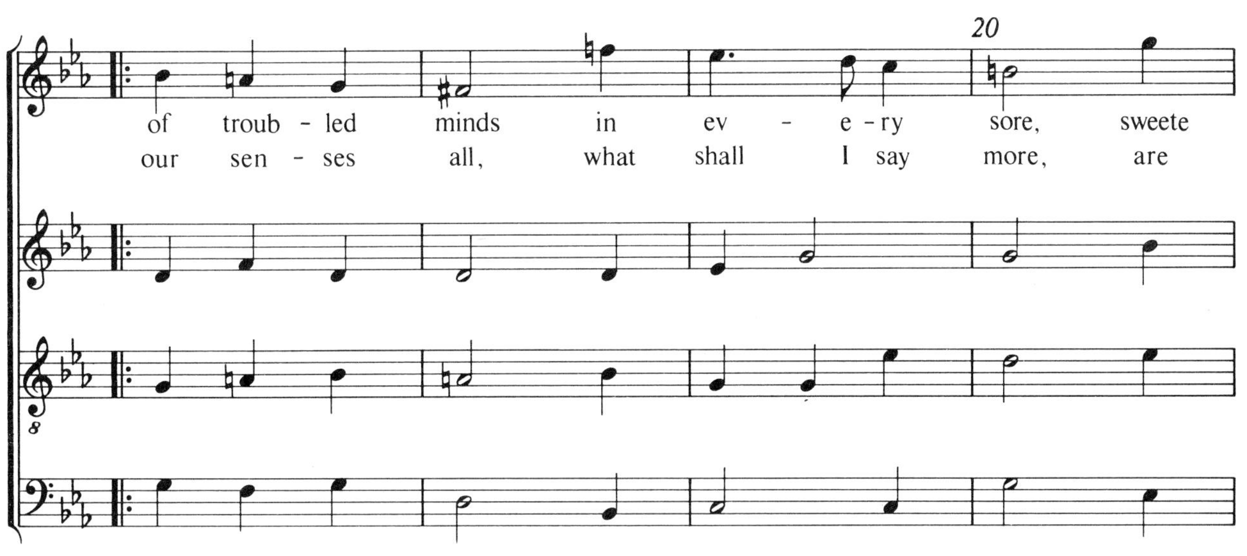
20
of troub - led minds in ev - e - ry sore, sweete
our sen - ses all, what shall I say more, are

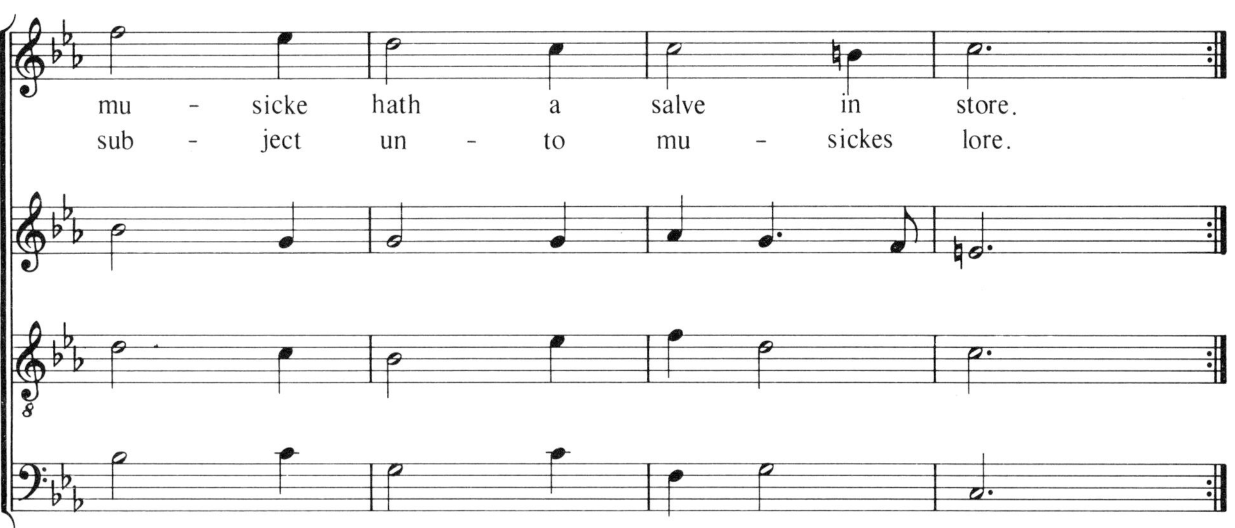
mu - sicke hath a salve in store.
sub - ject un - to mu - sickes lore.

25. *Shooting of the guns pavan* Anon.

With such an imposing title we might expect nothing short of a twenty-one-gun salute. Unfortunately five viols never sound impressively martial, though they do sound dignified and, particularly in a formal pavan, bring an air of ceremony and restraint. The origin of the title and the occasion of naming this pavan are unknown, but there is a theory that some instrumental works of the period were named after well-known galleons! Is a launching ceremony behind this innocent little dance? If so, cornetts and sackbutts would be more appropriate than retiring viols, despite the manuscript favouring viols. The pavan may be dated around 1580 and belongs stylistically to the first phase of English Renaissance instrumental ensemble music, whose characteristics are simplicity, homophony and formality. This style is that from which Holborne, Dowland and Ferrabosco developed their intricate approach to part-writing and its very severity provided a good master in the art of counterpoint.

Instrumentation

The lute part is entirely editorial, being simply a short score of the four lower parts with a decorated repeat in the style of written-out elaborate lute divisions, which gives nothing more than a skilled lutenist of the period could have improvised. The lute part can be omitted entirely. Judging from the manuscript source of the piece, the obvious instrumentation is a consort of viols but, as has been suggested, two cornetts and three sackbutts could be equally close to the original intentions. A consort of recorders could also be used.

Suggestions for interpretation

One of the biggest problems, whatever instruments are used, in such rhythmically bare part-writing is the ensemble discipline of moving precisely together. The first bar, for example, provides immense *basic* ensemble problems. Last bars of each section are very difficult to control, although the lute part helps to mark the beat. Care must be taken at the beginning of each section and repeats also tend to be ragged. The simplicity is beguiling, and this pavan can be used for improving any ensemble's ensemble no matter how superior it may feel.

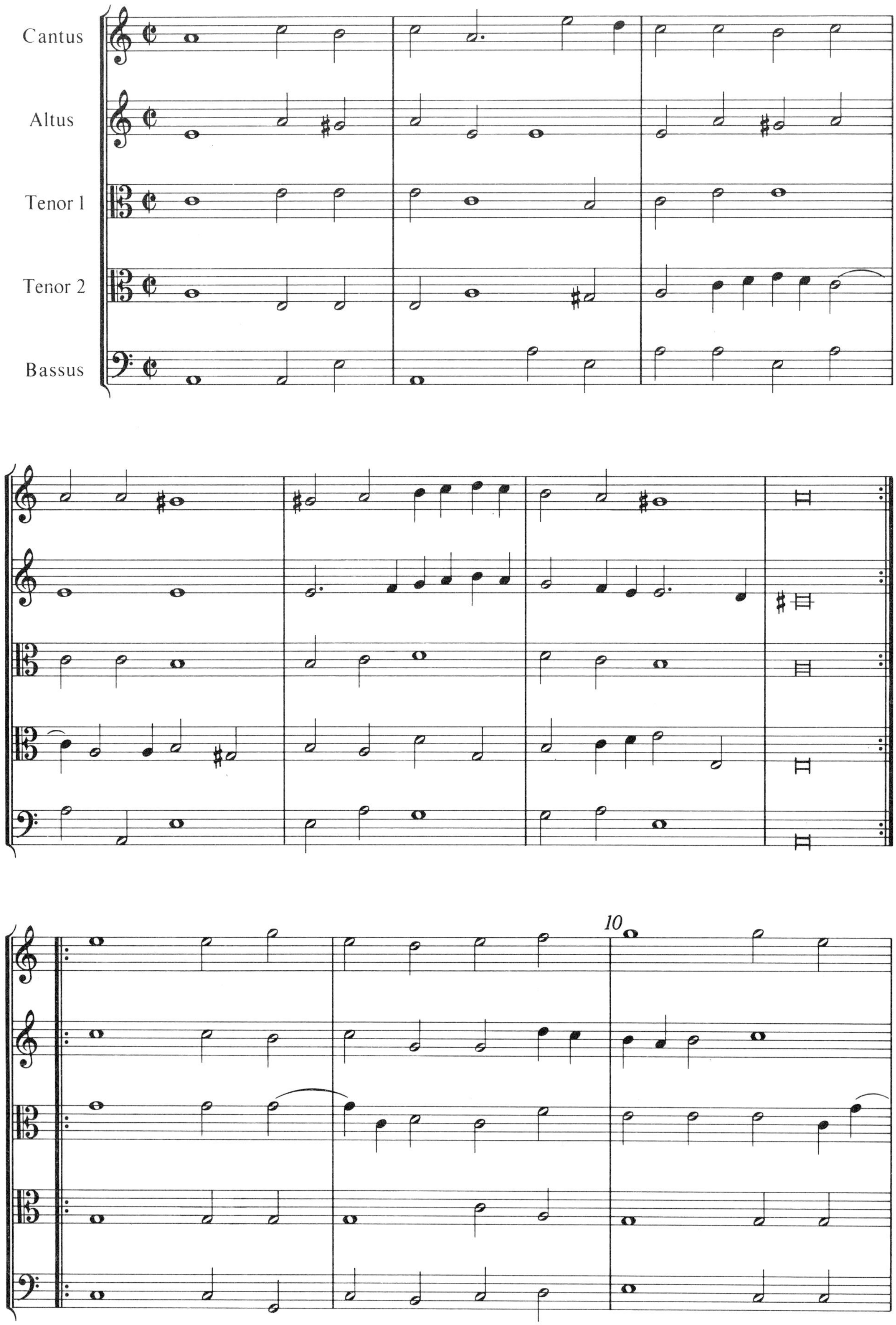

Cantus

Altus

Tenor 1

Tenor 2

Bassus

20

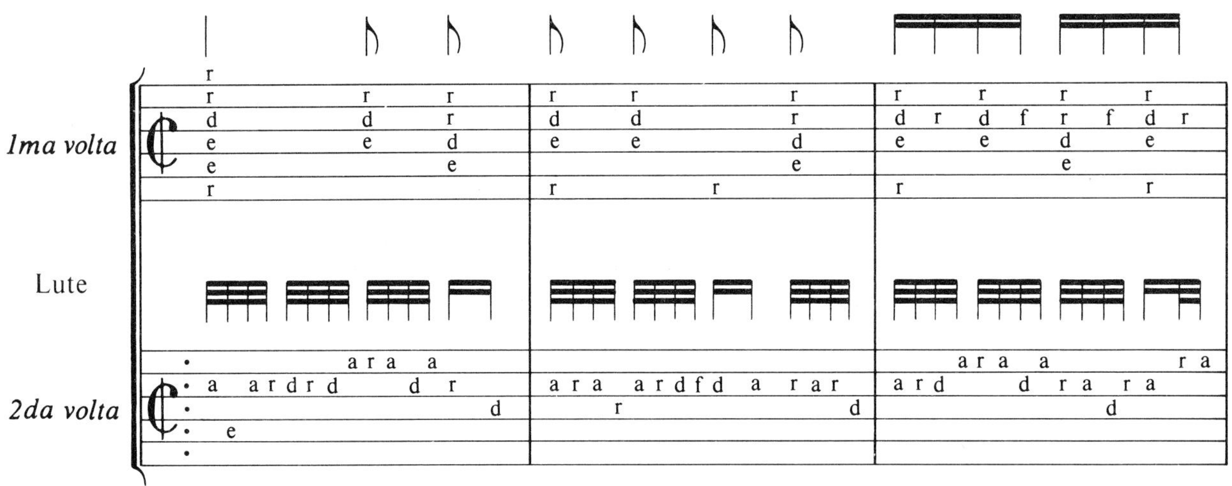
1ma volta
Lute
2da volta

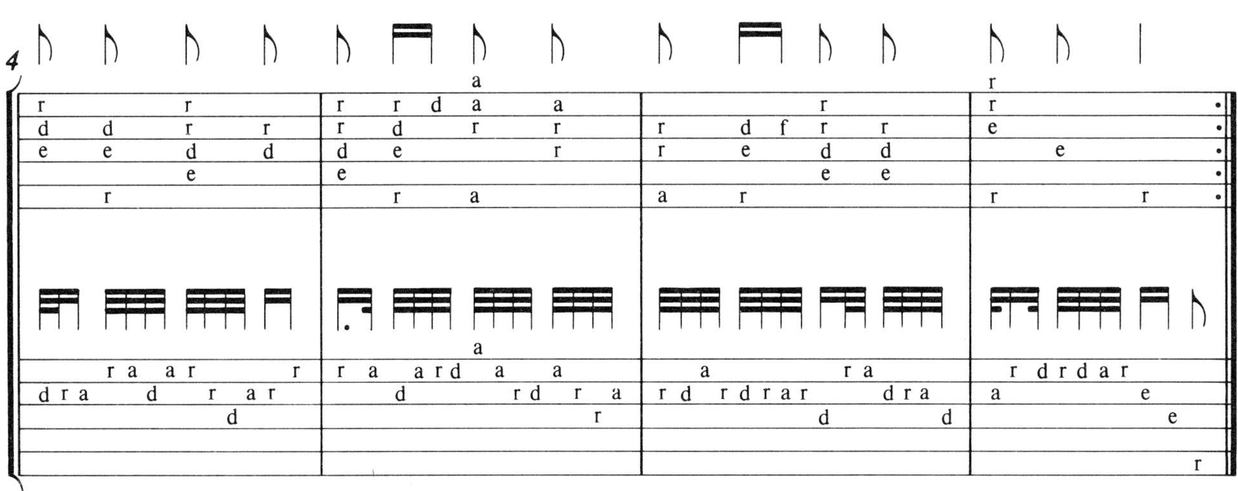
4

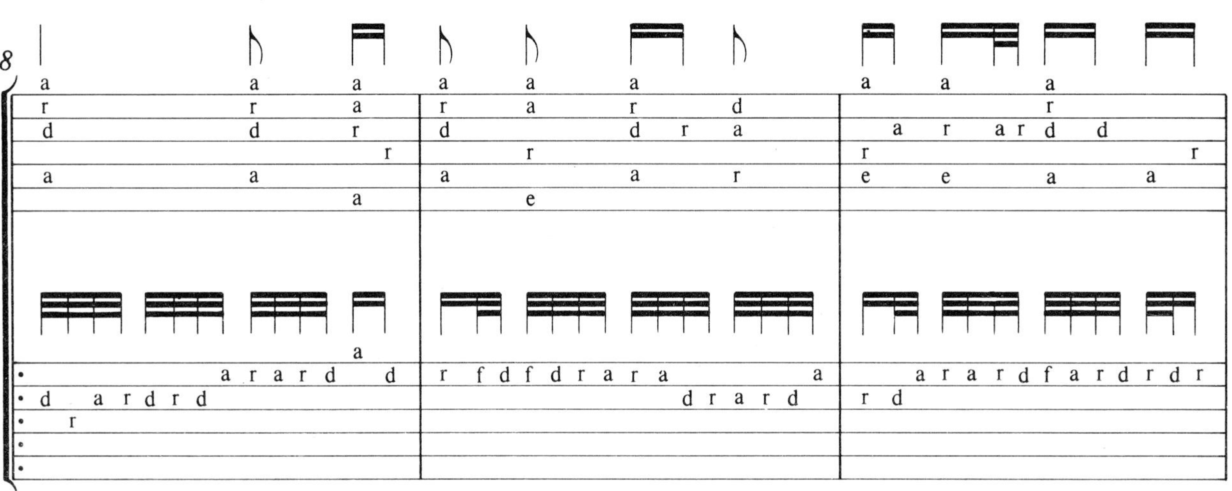
8

11

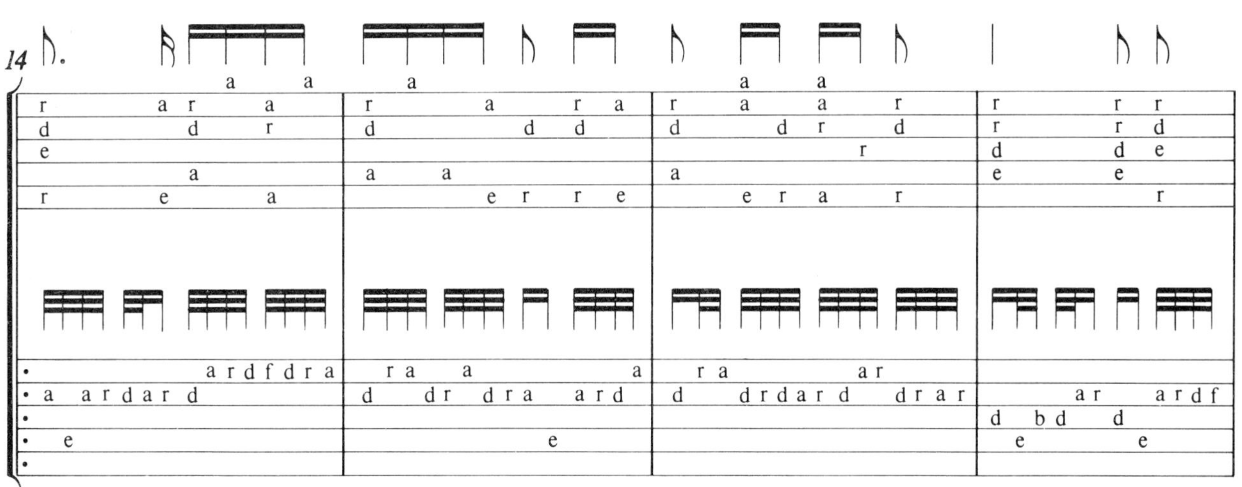

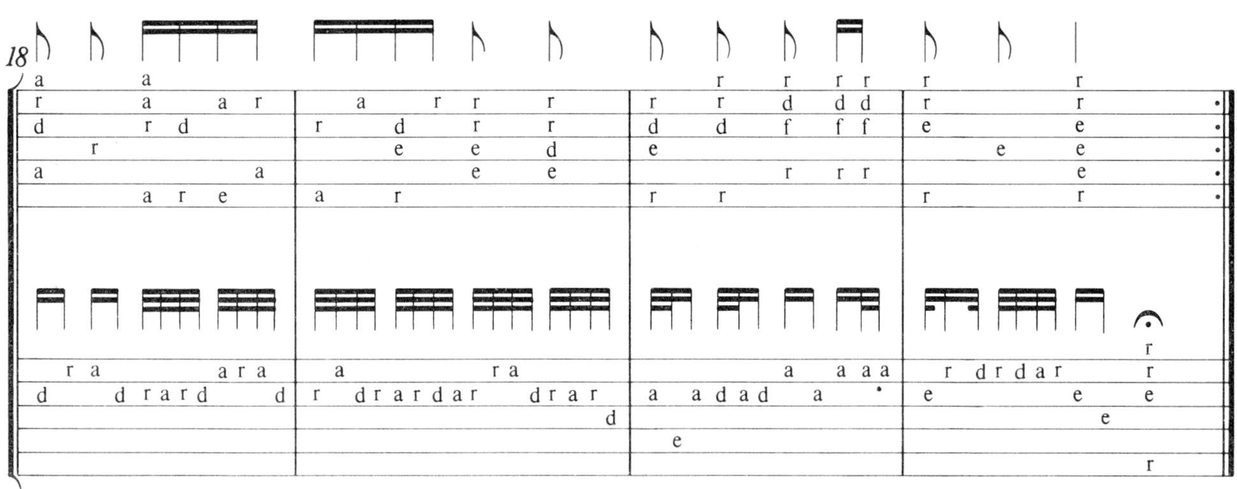

Glossary

The following is a list of terms used during the course of the book without explanation which may be unfamiliar to the non-specialist musician; some amplification may clarify certain points. The description of a term given here only suggests the particular meaning as used in this book. Some words have further meanings, some explanations need further expansion, some topics need detailed study for full comprehension. The reader is urged to refer to a more ample dictionary of music if any confusion remains. *The Harvard Dictionary of Music* by Willi Apel is very sound and includes most specialist terms found in early music.

a capella style of performance using voices alone, without instrumental accompaniment

arioso flowing melodic vocal style developed in Italy in the early seventeenth century in contrast to the more spoken, declamatory style cultivated at the same time

ballata see *frottola*

balli Italian dances of the mid-fifteenth century whose steps are preserved in several manuscripts compiled at that time. The dances are notable for their dramatic use of floor space in an original manner, very different from the contemporary French dance style

barzaletta see *frottola*

basse danse the most widespread court dance of the fifteenth century. A formal and serious dance cultivated differently in France and Italy

basso continuo accompaniment on a chordal instrument (lute family or keyboard) which is improvised by the player from the bass line. He provides the appropriate harmonies or 'realizes' the bass line. Developed in Italy at the end of the sixteenth century to accompany the new dramatic music for voice and later for instruments. The accompaniment should support the soloist(s) without intruding

basso seguente accompaniment of part-music on a chordal instrument by following the lines of each part exactly (as opposed to the improvised *continuo* style)

cantus firmus sometimes known as the 'tenor', it is the structural and architectural backbone of much fifteenth-century music. The *cantus firmus* is either composed first or already exists and is often in longer, slower notes than the other parts. The *cantus* and 'contratenor' are composed 'around' the *cantus firmus*, which remains the central reference point

canzona francese an Italian instrumental style which emerged in the 1560s. Presumably so called because it was influenced by the French *chanson* as opposed to the Italian madrigal, though why it should be used to refer to an instrumental genre is something of a mystery. Andrea and Giovanni Gabrieli wrote some of the finest music in this imposing style

chanson the basic general term for a secular composition primarily intended to be sung though may also be played instrumentally. Particularly applicable to the French vocal music

chitarrone a member of the lute family characterized by a long extension neck and pegbox and extra bass strings extending the range from a normal six-course lute down an octave. Variations in size, tuning and stringing specifications were numerous. Developed initially to increase the dramatic effectiveness of the accompaniment to Italian monody

cittern Italian cousin to the lute, strung with wire strings and played invariably with a plectrum. Several variant tunings and stringing specifications were in use

cornemuse a reed-cap instrument described in Praetorius (the great contemporary chronicler of musical instruments). A quiet buzzing sound characterizes the cornemuse

cornett a simple wind instrument with a cup-shaped mouthpiece capable of a wide dynamic range and considerable agility. Made of wood, straight or gently curved

crumhorn double-reed-mouthpiece wind instruments which give a characteristic bee-like buzz. The crumhorn family has a distinctive curl at the end of the narrow-bore tube

decoration see also *ornamentation*
addition to basic musical text, either written in by the composer, or improvised by the performer

divisions see also *ornamentation*
melodic decoration of intervals by use of smaller note-values than the basic melody. Most favoured form of ornamentation in the Renaissance period

fantasy see also *ricercare*
the most elaborate and extensive musical form for abstract (i.e. non-dance) instrumental music. But as the name implies the 'form' is created for each new piece, being tied to nothing but the inventive skill of the composer. Sections of polyphony and tight imitation contrast with looser, more rhapsodic material. The name 'ricercare' is somewhat interchangeable with 'fantasia' though less so as the sixteenth century progresses

ficta the practice of applying *musica ficta* to a melodic line, according to variable rules depending on context, was widely used in the sixteenth century. The term 'colouring' was also used for this process of raising or flattening a note from F to F♯, B to B♭ and so forth. The process was used to make the melodic contour more felicitous, according to taste, area and time. Much study is required before *ficta* can be applied with real authority

figured bass bass line of a composition with added numbers, which indicated the desired harmonic progressions and chord spacings necessary to complete the harmony. Early seventeenth-century practice, used as a kind of shorthand, which became increasingly important through the century

flute the flute in the text always means the one-piece keyless flute used in the Renaissance period. Various sizes were in use depending on the range of the part to be played, as in the recorder family. The most popular wind instrument for Renaissance chamber or domestic music

formes fixées the set poetic forms hallowed by medieval traditions which therefore enforced fixed musical forms when these texts were set. The *rondeau* is by far the most important of these

frottola meaning literally 'medley' or 'mixture' with popular overtones. A genre of Italian vocal music with instrumental accompaniment which was cultivated at court at the end of the fifteenth century. The style of writing was simple and mainly non-imitative, unlike the Flemish polyphony that flourished in Italy at the same time. Various poetic forms created a whole series of barely distinguishable musical forms under the generic label *frottola*. The similarities are such that one merges into another and it takes a specialist to distinguish with certainty a *ballata*, *barzaletta*, *sonetto* or *strambotto*, amongst numerous others. The music, though simple, is extremely refined within an overtly popular framework and was always in service to the poetry. Some of the best works use texts by Francesco Petrarch (1304–74), who was held as a model for contemporary poets

gittern the Renaissance guitar was a simple four-course instrument (later with five courses, *c.* 1590–1600), mainly used for simple dance music and popular songs. Some publications included abstract fantasias and extended the resources of this simple, but attractive, instrument to its limits. It was strummed or plucked with the fingers like the lute

gross-geigen see also *rebec*
term for rebec used in German treatises such as that by Hans Gerle

hexachord term for the system of naming the tones, only the first six notes of our eight-note scale system being named. *Ut, re, mi, fa, sol, la* were the syllables (known as solmization syllables). The lowest, *ut*, was placed on the G at the bottom of the bass clef and called *gamma ut*, the foundation note of the whole 'gamut' of the musical scale within man's singing range. All notes were labelled upwards to the E above the C above middle C by an intricate system called 'mutation', moving from one hexachord pattern to another. Interested readers should look at the simple and easily comprehensible table in, for example, Thomas Morley's *Plaine and Easie Introduction to Practical Musicke*, 1597 (facsimile edition available)

homophony style of part-writing using mono-rhythmic movement in all parts, creating block chords, and contrasting with polyphony, where each part has independent rhythmic movement

intabulation the practice of setting original vocal compositions in several parts for a single instrument (usually one of the lute family, sometimes a keyboard instrument). The term arises from the two styles of notation: mensural notation for part-music, tablature (a diagrammatic system) for lutes, citterns, gitterns and keyboard, etc. Hence 'to intabulate'

lute family see also *theorbo*; *chitarrone*
the pear shape, carved rose and several paired gut strings ('courses') sets the lute apart from other hand-plucked instruments (e.g. citterns and gitterns).

The lute occupied the highest place in Renaissance esteem for musical instruments, second only to the voice. It was a spur to poetic imagination and its best performers were treated with special respect. Its sixteenth-century solo repertoire is vast and its use in ensemble widespread. Like many Renaissance instrument types the lute came in a variety of sizes, from treble to bass. Numbers of strings varied, chronology being indicated by the number of strings required – five courses in 1480; six in 1500; seven by 1590; ten and more by 1620. During the seventeenth century the lute underwent many developments, hence the theorbo, chitarrone and such like. Tunings varied enormously, but for the whole period covered by this present collection the top six courses had the tuning relationships of (from the top) 4th, 4th, 3rd, 4th, 4th, with lower strings being adjustable, according to requirements. The most common pitch (nominal) was for an 'A'-tuned lute in Italy *c.* 1500–80; a 'G'-tuned lute in England *c.* 1580–1620. Most modern transcriptions take the 'G' tuning as standard

lyra da braccio bowed instrument especially designed for playing simple chords. Used almost exclusively for accompanying the voice, particularly self-accompaniment. Developed during the humanist revival in fifteenth-century Italy to emulate the performances of Orpheus, whose fabled singing and self-accompaniment was a constant source of inspiration in the Renaissance period. No music survives *specifically* for the *lyra da braccio* – it was always associated with courtly improvisation *melisma* the decoration of a plain melody (which moves note-for-note with each syllable of the poetry) by extending a syllable over several notes, often of a smaller note-value than the surrounding rhythmic movement. This creates a sweet and flowing effect, more *legato* than the general syllabic style

ornamentation see also *divisions, decoration, trill*

most sources of Renaissance music, printed or manuscript, present a plain text. But our knowledge of performance practices of the time suggests that extensive elaboration was brought to the plain versions made by the composer. This practice is called ornamentation or embellishment and is an area of study difficult to master. Ornamentation practices were so varied, depending so much on taste, time and location, that one cannot be sure of getting it right. But the effort should be made, for it is clear that good ornamentation was a highly prized feature of musical performance. The major features fall into two categories: divisions (or *passaggi*) and graces (trills, turns, etc.). The interested reader is urged to follow this subject in depth, for it is a constantly recurring, re-vitalizing feature of early music performance

passamezzo antico this title indicates not a tune but a harmonic sequence, a Renaissance twelve-bar blues, which is the basis for improvisation. The bass-line is:

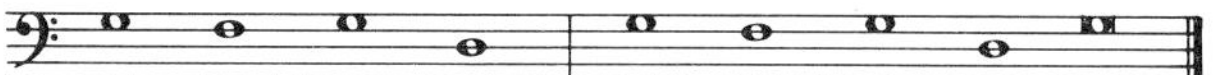

The *passamezzo antico* is one of a series of such harmonic sequences (or 'grounds', to use the Elizabethan term) which provided a musical *'lingua franca'* across Europe and across all social levels. Many composed settings of these 'grounds' survive, but their main use was as improvisational reference points. Their simplicity gives even the complete beginner an opportunity to improvise, whilst divisions can challenge the most advanced player. Such music is an ideal source of educational material, as well as being good fun

pavan a duple-measure dance in three sections, each of which is repeated. Perhaps the most refined dance of the sixteenth century, used for procession or when a mood of gravity was required. The early sixteenth-century Italian *pavana* was not quite as sober and was more probably used as an opportunity for preening and display – the word *pavana* derives from the word for 'peacock' and perhaps the strutting of the courting male should be imitated!

pitch a standard pitch (A 440 or any other) is a modern concept. A Renaissance 'G' was nominal, for it could have sounded anywhere between our F and A. In addition, transposition was applied automatically in many circumstances. Instruments of a fixed pitch (wind instruments, organ, etc.) dictated the pitch in a particular locality, otherwise the decision on pitch depended mainly on using the middle range (the 'speaking' or 'natural' range) of whatever forces were being used. Nowadays the effectiveness of the performance should be the ultimate deciding factor. Further reading is essential in this subject. See, for example, various articles on pitch in relation to instruments in *The Galpin Society Journal* and *Early Music* magazine

piva a simple dance, in imitation of a rustic dance, which usually has a triple, jig-like metre. The word *piva* means either 'point' (or 'round' dance?) or 'bagpipe' (or 'shepherds'' dance?). Either way, its rustic effect should be clear. The music should be played vigorously, in keeping with this mood

polyphony a style of composition in several parts, each of which has considerable rhythmic and melodic independence. Techniques of imitation, canon, inversions, etc. abound in the polyphonic style, which represents the highest achievements in medieval and Renaissance musical culture. The Renaissance period can be said to have ended, musically speaking, with the break-up of the 'seamless' polyphony which characterizes it. The *ars perfecta* of the Flemish composers *c.* 1500 (Josquin and his circle) provides the high point in a great tradition. Polyphony was created to echo the choiring angels singing God's praises, Man's attempt to raise his thoughts heavenward. Though the style was developed for the sacred mass and motet, it thoroughly suffused much secular composition, and even instrumental fantasias reflect the influence of polyphony

prolation a term which covers all the rhythmic species recognized by medieval music theory. Modern equivalents are approximately 2/4, 3/4, 6/8 and 9/8

quodlibet a composition which combines two or more texts or tunes from previously disparate sources. This musical 'game' was very popular at the end of the fifteenth century. Considerable skill was required to create what, in the end, is often a light-hearted joke

rauschpfeif a rather special form of shawm, but particularly loud. It has a double reed enclosed in a wind-cap

realization the specific term for the filling-out of a figured bass by adding the implied harmonies – one 'realizes' them

rebec a bowed instrument usually of three strings. Although used for refined musical performances in the mid-fifteenth century and earlier, by the sixteenth century the rebec had degenerated into a popular or folk instrument, spurned for use in 'art' music. The rebec came in non-standardized sizes and tunings but it is doubtful that a 'bass' rebec existed that could descend to the *'gamma ut'* at the bottom of the bass clef. More often the rebec is depicted held over-arm with a fairly short string length

recorder end-blown whistle-type mouthpiece, called flute in some countries. A family of recorders was in common use in the Renaissance period

ricercare meaning 'to search out', hence the feeling of improvisation. The earliest instrumental *ricercari* have a prelude-like feeling of searching, creating a mood, and were probably used as preludes, interludes or postludes in the performance of a song. By the end of the sixteenth century *ricercari* are usually longer, more structured and often display great ingenuity with polyphonic techniques of imitation, etc. The word 'fantasy' is more or less interchangeable with *ricercare*

rondeau the most important of the fifteenth-century *formes fixées*; it refers to the poetic form rather than the musical form, which must follow the poetic pattern. Careful juxtaposition of text repetition between new material creates a 'spun-out' unfolding of what often appears to us as a simple, clichéed idea. The most subtle variations of well-known themes obviously delighted the fifteenth-century listener intensely.

A1 B1 A2 A1 A3 B2 A1 B1 is the full pattern, where 'A' and 'B' represent the repeating text with A2 and B2 presenting new material within the scheme of the original 'A' and 'B'. The music is constructed as A and B and simply repeats this binary structure as appropriate.

The finest *rondeaux* create a bewitching atmosphere, which is achieved by the repetitions gathering a greater intensity as the scheme unfolds

sackbutt the sixteenth-century forerunner to the trombone, having a similar appearance, but more delicate with a narrower bore and smaller bell

shawm reed instrument with a conical bore and a loud, piercing tone. Used for outdoor music

si placet term given to the fourth, optional, part added to a three-part composition of the late fifteenth century. The fourth part might be by the original composer or by someone else

solmization see also *hexachord*
the use of the syllables *ut, re, mi, fa, sol, la* to name the notes of the hexachord as an aid in sight-singing and memory

sonetto see *frottola*

strambotto see *frottola*

tabor large double-headed drum held at the waist by a shoulder-strap, and beaten with a stick. One skin usually has a snare attached. Used for dancing in conjunction with a small pipe which can be played with one hand whilst the other beats the drum

tactus fundamental rhythmic unit which is then subdivided into small rhythmic units and patterns. The unchanging *tactus* provided a constant reference point in changes between duple and triple proportions

theorbo see also *lute*
member of the lute family, with extended range in the bass. A second extension neck continues from the normal pegbox, as in the *chitarrone*, allowing for the compass of bass strings. Used widely for vocal accompaniment and *continuo* playing

trill see also *ornamentation*
the decoration of a melodic note by 'gracing' rather than by 'divisions'. The main note is approached, or quitted, by lightly touching neighbouring notes. Various patterns were used, and given a variety of names such as trill, shake, fall, etc.

vers mesuré French poetry which is heavily influenced by classical metre, accent and construction. Experiments in such studied uses of the French language were encouraged by the various Academies flourishing in the 1570s, especially around the poets Ronsard and Baïf. The poetry was set to music, following supposed classical practice, where the poetic accent dictated the phrase length and melodic rise and fall

vielle bowed instrument, usually having three strings and waisted sides as in the violin family. It may be regarded as a forerunner of the modern violin. The *vielle* as such was obsolete by the end of the fifteenth century. Its tuning is conjectural, but 'fifths' were no doubt one system in common use

villancico a popular style of song-writing in Spain throughout the sixteenth century. Similar to the Italian *frottola* in function and usage

villotta a crude form of four-part vocal writing, in imitation of Italian street music. The simple style has vigour and charm, though many of the texts are coarse. The *villotta* may be regarded as the simplest style stemming from the *frottola*. Books of *villotte* were published in Italy in the 1540s

viol family the favoured bowed instruments of the sixteenth century, commonly used in various sizes, from treble to bass. The instruments were played between the knees, hence the term *viola da gamba*. The tuning, like the lute, is in fourths about a central third. The bowing action is light, with the bow held underhand, and a very graceful style of playing is possible which blends well with the voice or lute. Viol consorts (four, five or six together) were particularly cultivated in England from the end of the sixteenth century almost to the end of the seventeenth century

voix de villes songs written in a consciously rustic style, combining the grace of the court with country simplicity. French poets (Ronsard and others) lauded the pastoral life and wrote verse as though from the mouths of shepherds. These poems were anonymously set to pseudo folk-tunes and gathered in volumes to delight the court

Further reading

General histories and reference

Willi Apel, *Harvard Dictionary of Music*, Harvard University Press, 1970
Howard Mayer Brown, *Music in the Renaissance*, Prentice-Hall History of Music Series, 1976
'Ars Nova and the Renaissance (1300–1540)', *New Oxford History of Music Vol. III*, Oxford University Press, 1960
'The Age of Humanism (1540–1630)', *New Oxford History of Music Vol. IV*, Oxford University Press, 1968
Gustav Reese, *Music in the Renaissance*, Norton, 1954

Sixteenth-century writers

Baldassare Castiglione, *The Booke of the Courtier* (English translation by Sir Thomas Hoby, 1561), Dent & Sons, 1975
Thomas Morley, *A Plaine and Easie Introduction to Practicall Musicke* (modern facsimile of 1597 edition), Dent & Sons, 1952 and later reprints
J. M. Osborne, *The Autobiography of Thomas Whythorne*, Oxford University Press, 1962
O. Strunk, *Source Readings in Music History: The Renaissance*, Norton, 1965

Books on musical instruments

Jeremy Montagu, *The World of Medieval and Renaissance Musical Instruments*, David and Charles, 1976
David Munrow, *The World of Early Musical Instruments* (book and set of records), Oxford University Press, 1975
Mary Remnant, *Musical Instruments of the West*, Batsford, 1978

Magazines

'Early Music', edited by J. M. Thomson and published quarterly by Oxford University Press

Societies, etc.

The Lute Society: 29 St Donatt's Road, New Cross, London SE14
The Viola da Gamba Society: 93A Sutton Road, London N10
The Society of Recorder Players: 31 Milford Gardens, Edgware, Middlesex
The Galpin Society: 116 Tennison Road, Cambridge
The Early Music Centre: 62 Princedale Road, London W11

The above societies produce publications and journals, take members, organize meetings and summer schools, and provide information to the general public

Useful handbooks

Brian Jeffries, *Belle Buche e Belle Parlure* (a guide to the pronunciation of early French), Tecla Editions, 1976

Howard Mayer Brown, *Ornamentation of the Sixteenth Century*, Oxford University Press, 1976

Anthony Rooley, *A New Variety of Lute Lessons* (book of music and record, with introduction to tablature for guitarists), Guitar Magazine Publications, 1976

Recordings

'The World of Early Music', The Consort of Musicke (Dir. Anthony Rooley), Decca Records, Oiseau Lyre *Florilegium* (DSLO 12 BB203–6). complete recording of the present selection of music

'Musicke of Sundrie Kindes', The Consort of Musicke (Dir. Anthony Rooley), Decca Records, Oiseau Lyre *Florilegium* (DSLO 12BB203–6). A four-record set including all the present selection and many more pieces

More about Penguins and Pelicans

For further information about books available from Penguins please write to Dept EP, Penguin Books Ltd, Harmondsworth, Middlesex UB7 ODA.

In the U.S.A.: For a complete list of books available from Penguins in the United States write to Dept CS, Penguin Books, 625 Madison Avenue, New York, New York 10027

In Canada: For a complete list of books available from Penguins in Canada write to Penguin Books Canada Ltd. 2801 John Street, Markham, Ontario L3R 1B4.

In Australia: For a complete list of books available from Penguins in Australia write to the Marketing Department, Penguin Books Australia Ltd, P.O. Box 257, Ringwood, Victoria 3134.

The Penguin Book of English Madrigals: for four voices

EDITED BY DENIS STEVENS

Twenty-nine works picked from the cream of the repertory for four voices.

The Penguin Book of English Madrigals: for five voices

EDITED BY DENIS STEVENS

Twenty-one of the finest five-part madrigals.

The Penguin Book of Italian Madrigals

EDITED BY JEROME ROCHE

Thirty-two pieces drawn from the earlier part of the golden age of Italian madrigals in the sixteenth century. There is a guide to pronunciation, and a prose translation of each madrigal.

The Penguin Book of English Folk Songs

EDITED BY RALPH WILLIAMS AND A. L. LLOYD

A classic collection of the rarer songs.

The Penguin Book of Christmas Carols

EDITED BY ELIZABETH POSTON

Fifty carols, for which Elizabeth Poston has herself arranged the music, providing each with a simple vocal or instrumental descant. The carols range from *Hark, the Herald Angels* to folk carols from France and Russia.

The Second Penguin Book of Christmas Carols

EDITED BY ELIZABETH POSTON

A collection focussing on the American contribution to the genre, from Negro slave-music to White folk-song and hymnody.